CONTENTS

AMAZING CARS	6
About Cars	7
Smart Fortwo	8
Tesla Roadster	10
Ariel Atom 500	12
Mayback 62	14
Bugatti Veyron	16
Ultimate Aero TT	18
The RoadRazer	20
Mercedes-Benz F400	22
SLK 55 AMG	24
Mercedes-Benz SLR McLaren	26
Gumpert Apollo	28
Artega GT	30
KTM X-Bow	32
Audi R8	34

AMAZING BIKES	36
About Motorcycles	37
Ducati 1098R	38
Ducati Superbike 749	40
Ducati 999S	42
Honda CBR1000RR	44
Honda Shadow Spirit 750 C2	46
Kawasaki Ninja ZX-10R	48
Kawasaki Vulcan 900 Custom	50
BMW K1200LT	52
BMW Cruiser R 1200 C Montauk	54
BMW K1200S	56
BMW R1200R	58
BMW R1150RS	60
Big Dog K-9	62
MTT Turbine	64

Copyright: North Parade Publishing Ltd.
4 North Parade, Bath, BA1 1LF, UK

First Published: 2010
All rights reserved. No part of this publication may be reprinted, stored in a retrieval system or transmitted, in any form or by any means, electronic, mechanical, photocopying, recording, or otherwise, without the prior permission of the copyright holder.

CONTENTS

DIGGERS, TRUCKS & EARTH MOVERS	**66**
Hydraulics at Work	67
Bulldozers	68
Loaders	70
Diggers	72
Draglines	74
Cranes	76
Crane Mania	78
Scrapers	80
Trucks	82
Dump Trucks	84
Mixers	86
Snowplough	88
Road Construction	90
Forestry Vehicles	92
COMBAT AIRCRAFT	**94**
Know Your Combat Aircraft	95
World War I Fighters	96
European Bombers of WWII	98
The Attack on Pearl Harbour	100
Enter the Americans	102
Flying into the Jet Age	104
Supersonic Fighters	106
Supersonic Bombers	108
Modern Combat Aircraft	110
Naval Combat Aircraft	112
Helicopters in Combat	114
American Combat Helicopters	116
European Combat Helicopters	118
Combat Aircraft of the Future	120
Glossary	122
Index	124

ABOUT CARS

Karl Benz invented the first car in 1885. This car had three wheels and was powered by a petrol engine.

What's in this book?

Since then cars have evolved into the four wheeled wonders of today, where cars of many different shapes and sizes are available. This book will introduce you to three main types of amazing cars.

Super Cars

Super cars are high end sports cars with extremely powerful engines. They are designed for speed and performance and are luxury items that usually come with a hefty price tag!

Sports Cars

Sports cars typically have lowered suspension, powerful engines and a streamlined body. They are designed for high speeds and good cornering, usually with stiffer suspension.

Cars today are ever more daring and unique in their design.

Street Cars

As the name suggests, street cars are utility vehicles that operate on roads. With rising oil prices, automobile companies are increasingly looking to more economical and smaller street cars to meet demand.

 Performance cars stand out with their sleek and aerodynamic designs.

Did You Know?

Almost 100,000 patents have been registered by inventors in the evolutionary history of the car.

SMART FORTWO

They say that good things come in small packages. The Smart Fortwo is a perfect example of this.

Two Seater

The Smart Fortwo is a smart and compact two-seater car. The car was first displayed at the 1998 Paris Motor Show. At the time, the car was named the City Coupe. The car was **modified** and relaunched as a second generation in early 2008.

 The compact design of the Fortwo means it can zip through small spaces.

Fits Anywhere

The Smart Fortwo is 2.69 metres (m) long, equal to the width of a truck or a regular parking slot. This means that two or three Smarts can park side by side in a standard space reserved for a single car. This ability to fit in tight spaces alone means that the car is perfect for crowded city roads.

Did You Know?

The Fortwo is made of interchangeable body panels — so one car can easily assume a different look.

```
TECHNICAL INFO
Manufacturer: Smart
Type: Microcar
Engine: 1,000cc
0-60 mph: 10.9 sec
Top speed: 90 mph
```

 Despite its compact size the interior of the Smart is surprisingly spacious.

Sturdy Engine

The Smart Fortwo features an 84 bhp engine that powers the car from 0–60 mph in 10.9 seconds. The car can run for 60 miles on just 5.7 litres of petrol. The car comes with an automated 5-speed transmission. This means it can be operated manually or automatically, and even has a Formula One-style paddle gear change option.

 The Smart Fortwo features a compact engine mounted in the rear of the car.

TESLA ROADSTER

Imagine a sports car that runs only on electricity and releases no harmful gasses! The Tesla Roadster is the answer.

Electrifying Car

The Tesla Roadster is a high performance, electric sports car manufactured by Tesla Motors. This attractive-looking roadster was designed with the help of Lotus. The body of the car is designed in a special way to maximise efficiency and performance, using a structure made of carbon fibre and aluminium. For a jerk-free ride, Tesla has only two gears. It also has electrically controlled door handles, **airbags** and **anti-lock braking system**.

Did You Know?

The first known electric locomotive was built by Scottish inventor Robert Davidson in 1837.

The Tesla is based on a modified Lotus Elise body that was redesigned by Lotus engineers.

TECHNICAL INFO
Manufacturer: Tesla Motors
Car type: Roadster
0-60 mph: 3.9 sec
Top speed: 125 mph (electronically limited)

No Engine

As an electric car, the Tesla Roadster doesn't have an internal combustion engine. Instead, it has the Energy Storage System (ESS) which comprises of a 450 kg lithium ion battery. The 6,831 cells in the battery pack are enough to produce over 248 hp. The Tesla can cover around 240 miles without recharging. The lack of an engine means that the car is very silent.

Dream Machine

The Tesla breaks all the conventional images of an electric car with a smooth, sleek body. The car is fast and stylish, performing and handling like a sports car.

 The interior of the Tesla Roadster.

ARIEL ATOM 500

A sports car that has an inside-out look! The Ariel Atom 500's basic body structure is unlike any other sports car that you will have seen before.

Did You Know?
The Atom appears in video games such as Project Gotham Racing 3.

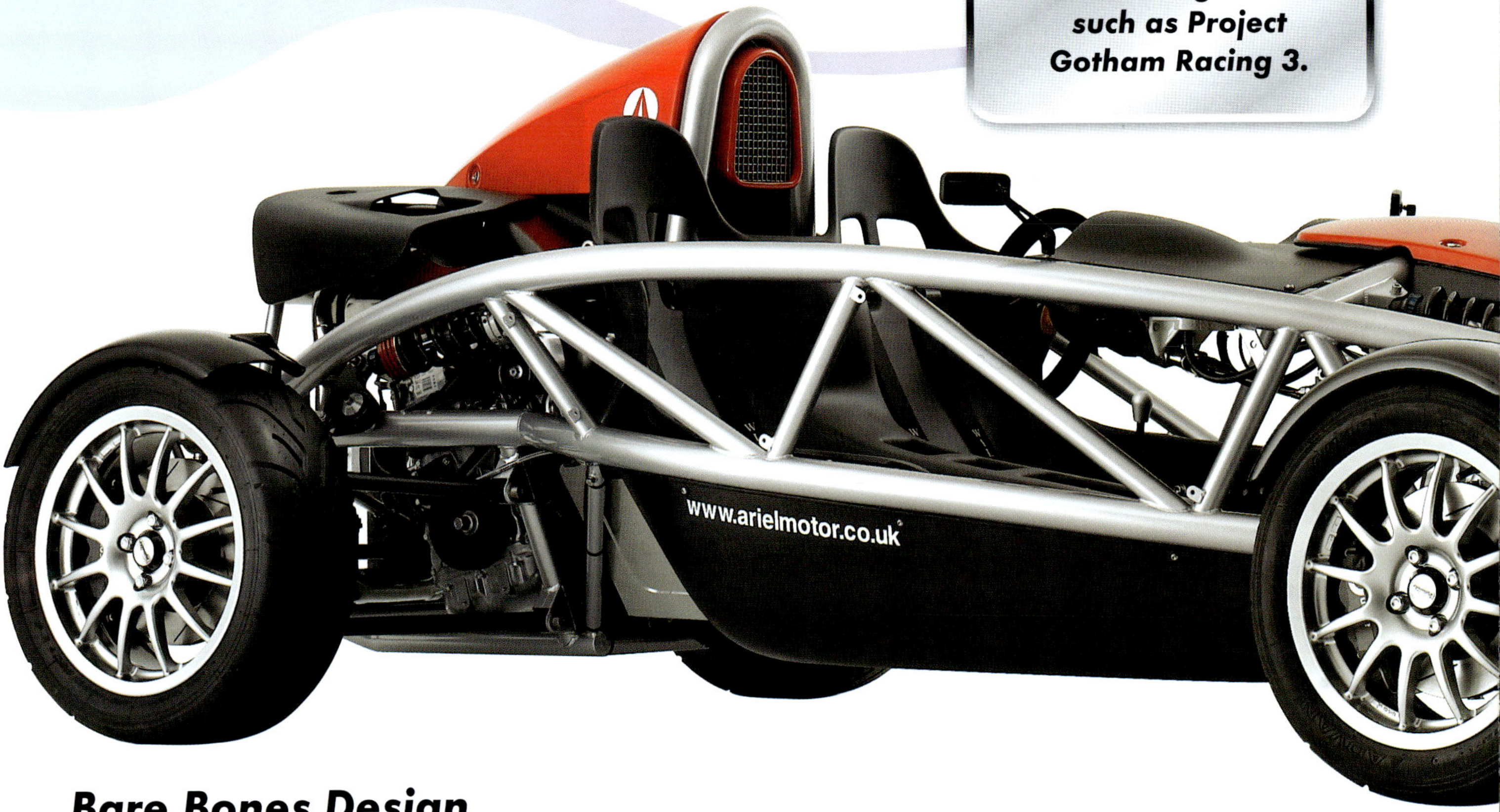

Bare Bones Design

The Ariel Atom is produced by England's Ariel Motor Company, and manufactured under license in USA by TMI Auto Tech Inc. With Formula One racing car looks, the Ariel Atom has a nose cone and an engine mounted just behind the driver. There are no doors, no roof and no windshield – so hold on to your hats!

The visible framework gives the Atom the look of a skeleton car.

Mean Machine

The Ariel Atom is available with a range of engine options, most notably the supercharged Honda Civic Type-R K20 and the General Motors Ecotec engine. The car's top speed is relatively tame compared to other sports cars. However, the lightweight design means the car is capable of tremendous acceleration. Moreover, rigid suspension allows for tight and fast cornering. What little bodywork there is comes in the form of separate panels. This reduces weight and the cost and allows for easy maintenance.

The engine is housed right behind the seating compartment.

The car can be described as no frills: it doesn't even have a stereo!

TECHNICAL INFO

Manufacturer: Ariel Motor Company
Car type: Sports car
Engine: 1,988 cc
0-60 mph: 2.9 sec
Top speed: 140 mph

MAYBACH 62

The Maybach 62 is a luxury 4-door car. Its length of 6.17 metres and princely design makes the car super spacious and elegant. Almost no luxury is spared, with the car including a glass roof, leather lined cabin, electric reclining seats and LCD display screens.

Did You Know?
The Maybach 62 weighs a massive 2,735kg, making it one of the heaviest production cars.

Power

The Maybach 62 has a twin-turbocharged V12 engine. This enables the car to reach a speed of 155 mph. The 612 hp engine can power the car from 0-60 mph in just 5.2 seconds. But the Maybach is designed for comfort and luxury so will rarely be driven at such speeds.

In the Lap of Luxury

A ride in the luxurious Maybach 62 is a rare experience. This luxury saloon showcases cutting edge technology and the highest comfort levels. For the rear passengers, the car has individual seats with total leg and foot support. For long journeys, two LCD screens with entertainment facilities are provided to keep away boredom. The **suspension** is even specially tuned for a more comfortable ride.

Every Maybach engine is hand-assembled.

The best thing about the Maybach 62 is that each one has its own unique specification.

TECHNICAL INFO
Manufacturer: Daimler AG
Car type: Luxury saloon
Engine: 5,513cc
0-60 mph: 5.2 sec
Top speed: 155 mph

BUGATTI VEYRON

Bugatti is one of the automotive industry's oldest brand names. Today the company is owned by Volkswagen and manufactures one of the fastest sports car in the world, the Bugatti Veyron.

Did You Know?

At full throttle the Veyron does just 2.46 miles per gallon of fuel!

The Bugatti Veyron

Volkswagen wanted to develop the most powerful car in the world. So they took a 1,001 hp engine and designed a car around it. Under the sleek body are the kinds of features more commonly seen on Formula One cars. Front and rear spoilers provide better control. Roof-mounted snorkels, the rear-deck vents and side-mounted scoops bring air to the engine and rear brakes.

The Veyron has the greatest acceleration of any production car ever made.

16

Engine

The Veyron has a massive 16-cylinder engine that delivers 1,001 **horsepower**. The engineers came up with a unique W-shaped design that allowed them to pack a lot of power into a compact design. To keep its weight down, the engine is made of aluminium and magnesium and has four turbochargers. The 7-gear system is computer-controlled, like those found in a Formula One car. There is no clutch pedal or shift lever — the computer controls the clutch disks as well as the actual shifting.

Interiors

The Veyron is a two seater, but it seats the two people in lavish style. The interior is covered almost completely in leather, from the dash to the doors. Only the instruments and a few metal details interrupt the opulent trim. The car also surrounds its occupants with every sort of electronic gadget, from a remarkable stereo system to a **navigation system**.

Almost every part of the Veyron's interior is covered in rich leather.

```
TECHNICAL INFO
Manufacturer: Volkswagen
Car type: Super car
Engine: 7,993cc
0-60 mph: 2.46 sec
Top speed: 253 mph
```

SSC ULTIMATE AERO TT

On September 13, 2007, the Ultimate Aero TT hit a top speed of 257 mph, making it the world's fastest production car!

Features

The Aero's body is made of carbon fibre and titanium to help reduce the weight of the car while keeping it strong. The car has a leather interior, 10-speaker system, a camera to assist with reversing, and even a hydraulic lift to help the car get over speed bumps!

Did You Know?

The SSC Ultimate Aero TT is one of the most powerful road cars in the world.

 The Aero has distinctive butterfly doors similar to the SLR McLaren and Enzo Ferrari.

The Ultimate Aero produces more emissions-legal horsepower than any other production car in the world.

Engine

The Aero has a massive 6.35 litre engine with a **displacement** of 6,345cc that produces 1,183 hp. The engine is twin-turbocharged, with a driver-operated boost.

THE ROADRAZER

The first thing that you will notice about the RoadRazer is its long snout. This two-seater car, which weighs just 300 kg, is one of the lightest road-legal sports cars available.

With its pointed nose cone the RoadRazer looks amazingly shark-like.

The Design

The RoadRazer was created by Mikkel Steen Pedersen, a motor racing enthusiast and engineer. The RoadRazer promises to deliver stunning levels of performance, thanks to the car's power-to-weight ratio, low centre of gravity and effective **aerodynamics**.

Engine

The RoadRazer has a converted 1,300**cc** Suzuki Hayabusa motorcycle engine. The engine produces approximately 175 hp, hitting 60 mph in just 3 seconds. Unlike most wet sump car engines, the RoadRazer has a dry sump oil pumping system.

```
TECHNICAL INFO
Manufacturer: RoadRazer
Car type: Sports car
Engine: 1,300cc
0-60 mph: 3 sec
```

The engine is rear-mounted, behind the tandem passenger seat.

Exterior and Interior

The RoadRazer has a racing seat for the driver positioned very close to the ground, like a true racing car. There is a passenger seat, but this is in a tandem arrangement just behind the driver, with the passenger placing their legs either side of the seat in front; not recommended for long journeys!

The raised nosecone position of the RoadRazer is designed not only to aid performance in cornering, but also to assist with day-to-day driving when parking and clearing speed-bumps etc. The curved side pods of the RoadRazer act like inverted aeroplane wings, pushing the car into the ground and affording grip and handling.

The car seats two people one behind the other, but the passenger must straddle the driver's seat with their legs!

MERCEDES-BENZ F 400

The Mercedes-Benz F 400 Carving is a concept car and research vehicle. Among several innovations, the car gets the last part of its name because of its ability to tilt its wheels inwards when cornering, carving like a ski or snowboard.

Design

The Carving is a triumph of innovative design and style. The engineers have mixed steel, aluminium and carbon fibre to make the car lightweight and yet sturdy. Perhaps the most distinctive elements of the design are the wing profile wheel arches that flare out to allow for the wheels to tilt in cornering.

 The F 400 Carving is packed with dynamic systems that are being tested for use in future production cars.

Did You Know?

The Carving uses new lighting technology: fibre optic wires transmit light from special lamps beneath the bonnet to the main headlamps.

Active Camber Control System

The system of tilting the F 400's wheels inwards when cornering is known as active camber control. According to Mercedes, this system gives 30 percent more lateral stability than conventional turning. The system is controlled by a computer that monitors driver inputs to the steering and will adjust the tilt, or camber, of the tyres automatically as needed to maximise grip and increase safety.

 When the car is cornering, the outer wheels tilt inwards, leaving only the inner area of these tyres in contact with the road.

 The car has the extended bonnet and short tail end of a classic roadster, but that's where the similarities end!

SLK 55 AMG

The Mercedes-Benz SLK 55 AMG is a stylish, high-performance roadster, having been tuned and modified from the standard SLK 55.

Powerhouse

Underneath the bonnet the SLK 55 AMG has a supercharged 5.5 litre V8 engine powering the car. The power is harnessed by a 7-speed gearbox controlled by shift paddles on the steering wheel. The car boasts the only V8 engine in its class and is capable of up to 6,700 rpm.

Did You Know?

AMG began tuning Mercedes cars over 30 years ago, before they were bought by the company.

The SLK 55 AMG is a roadster designed for track racing.

Interiors and Exteriors

The SLK 55 AMG can be converted into a coupe from a convertible and vice versa at the push of a button. The roof neatly folds away in just 16 seconds! Inside, the car comes with contoured sports seats in fine leather, as well as an ergonomically designed steering wheel, complete with paddle gear shift.

Safety First

AMG has gone to great lengths to ensure that the car is safer, quicker and cleaner than its predecessors. It has also worked at improving the aerodynamics of the car. Handling is assisted by state-of-the-art active body control, while high-performance disc brakes are fitted to both front and rear wheels.

The cabin of the SLK 55 AMG

TECHNICAL INFO

Manufacturer: Mercedes-Benz
Car type: Convertible
Engine: 5,439cc
0-60 mph: 4.8 sec
Top speed: 155 mph (electronically limited)

MERCEDES-BENZ SLR MCLAREN

As the name suggests the SLR McLaren is Formula One inspired in both its performance and its styling – indeed SLR stands for sport, light, racing! Ultimate performance and detailed styling combine to make the fastest road-legal convertible available today.

 The SLR has a 21st century take on the gullwing doors from the original Mercedes 300SL.

Amazing Roof System

Perhaps the most attractive feature of this roadster is the roof system. It has a z-fold roof which opens and closes in just 10 seconds. The roof is made from special hi-tech material that is designed to withstand the force created at high speeds, while insulating the cabin from the elements and noise.

Aerodynamics

The SLR features active aerodynamics. There is a spoiler mounted on the rear which automatically raises at speeds above 60 mph. This increases the downforce, helping to pin the rear of the car to the ground at high speeds.

Did You Know?

During testing, the SLR McLaren Roadster's roof was lowered and raised over 20,000 times to ensure its build quality.

Design

The SLR McLaren uses Triax carbon fibre for the body of the car. The brakes of the car are made of carbon ceramic that provide for optimum performance and control under braking. In the cockpit, carbon fibre and luxurious leather combine to evoke the feel of SLRs from previous decades.

GUMPERT APOLLO

The Gumpert Apollo is a road-legal high-performance sports car. The designers' vision was to produce a car with so much downforce, power and aerodynamic efficiency that it could technically drive upside-down!

Road Car Meets Track Car

The Gumpert Apollo is the perfect synthesis of a road vehicle and track car. According to the makers, the car generates a sense of passion and pleasure beyond all expectations. Noticeable racing-inspired features include the front lip air splitter and and roof-mounted triangular air intake.

TECHNICAL INFO
Manufacturer: Gumpert
Car type: Super car
Engine: 4,163cc
0-60 mph: 3.0 sec
Top speed: 224 mph

The car has striking gullwing doors.

Interiors

The inside of the Gumpert Apollo is compact and designed to be lightweight. The customer is then able to specify the interior features as they please. Options include air conditioning, music system and a backward facing camera to help with reversing. Seats are individually tailored to the customer with padding, upholstery and adjustable paddles. Every detail, right down to the colour of the seams and stitching, can be specified by the customer!

 The interior of the car is functional and lightweight.

Features

The Apollo has an Audi 4.2 litre V8 engine combined with a six-speed gearbox. The engine produces a respectable 650 hp that powers the car from 0-60 mph in just 3 seconds. A fibre glass frame and carbon fibre body panels mean that the car weighs in at just 1,200 kg. The car's wide and imposing wheel arches house impressive 19-inch aliminium-cast wheel rims.

 The Gumpert Apollo is built around an Audi V8 engine.

ARTEGA GT

The Artega GT is a mid-engined sports car designed by Henrik Fisker of Aston Martin DB9 fame. This compact car weighs only 1,100 kg, giving it an excellent power-to-weight ratio.

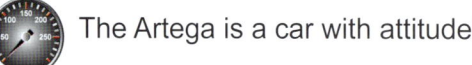 The Artega is a car with attitude!

 Agility, driving dynamics and safety were key factors in the design of the car.

Engine

The Artega is powered by a 3.6-litre Volkswagen-sourced V-6 engine. The engine produces 300 hp of power with a top speeds of 167 mph. **Acceleration** from 0-60 mph is expected to be under five seconds. The engine is placed horizontally in the rear.

Design

The hood and the headlights of the Artega GT stand out for their broad and distinctive design. The interior of the Artega is surprisingly spacious for a GT with its kind of power. Indeed, Artega boast that their car is the width of a luxury limousine!

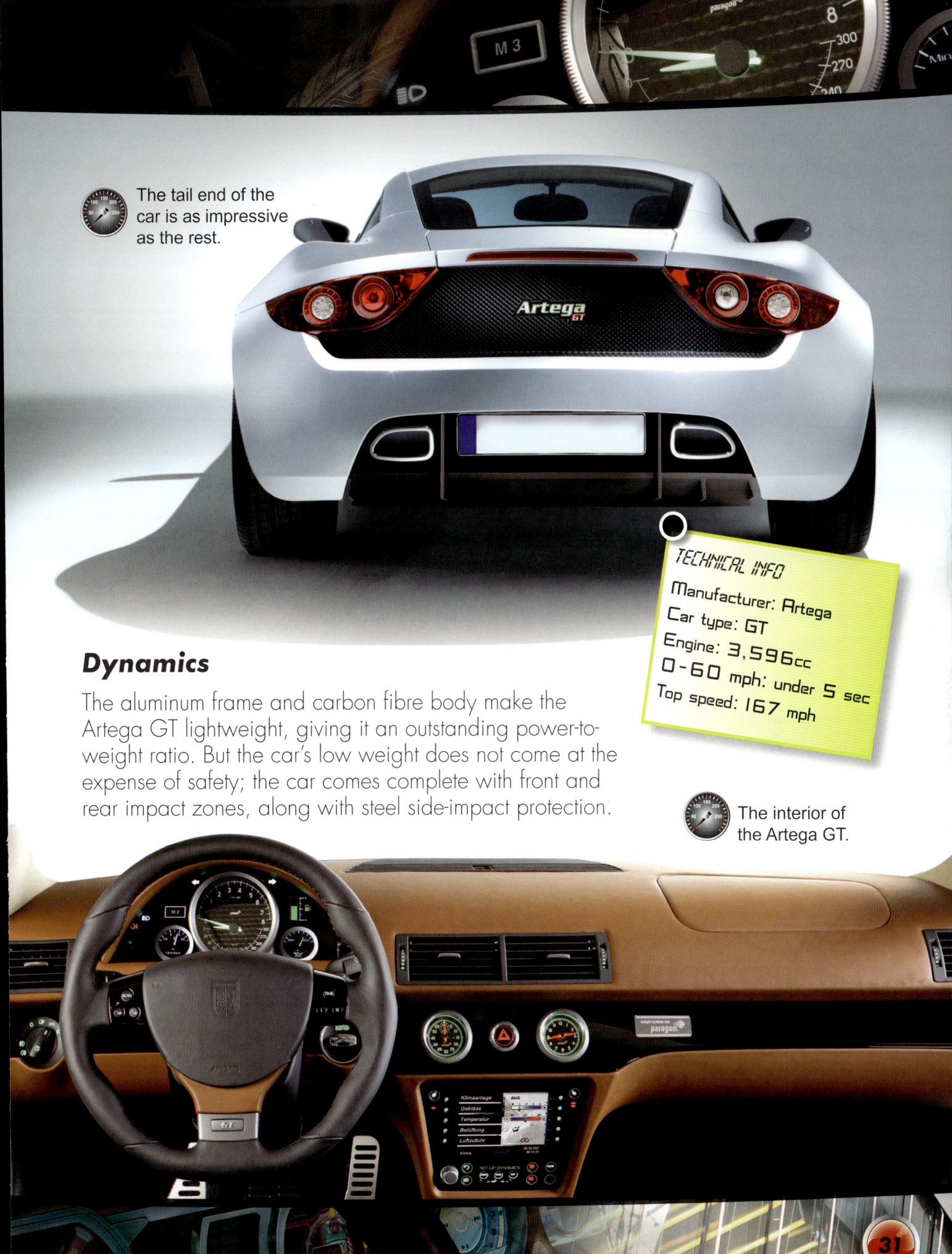

The tail end of the car is as impressive as the rest.

Dynamics

The aluminum frame and carbon fibre body make the Artega GT lightweight, giving it an outstanding power-to-weight ratio. But the car's low weight does not come at the expense of safety; the car comes complete with front and rear impact zones, along with steel side-impact protection.

```
TECHNICAL INFO
Manufacturer: Artega
Car type: GT
Engine: 3,596cc
0-60 mph: under 5 sec
Top speed: 167 mph
```

The interior of the Artega GT.

KTM X-BOW

The KTM X-Bow is the first car to be produced by motorcycle manufacturers KTM. By the maker's own admission, the X-Bow is an aggressively designed, radical, lightweight sports car.

Light But Fast

The X-Bow is powered by a 240 hp Audi TFSI engine that powers the car from 0-60 mph in just 3.9 seconds. The relatively small engine is capable of this because the car itself weighs in at just 790 kgs. This four-wheel pocket rocket is 144.5 inches long, 73.6 inches wide and just 45.7 inches high!

Did You Know?

The KTM X-Bow is made with Austrian design and money, a German engine, and Italian engineering.

Features

The KTM X-Bow doesn't have a roof, or even a windscreen, so a helmet is adviseable! The manufacturer has tried to develop a vehicle that combines the thrills of both bikes and cars. Built on the principles of racing technology, the wheels stand clear from the chassis, with exposed racing suspension. So stripped back and prepared for racing is this car that it doesn't even have any doors – you simply climb over the side to get in!

 Despite its pure racing design, the X-Bow is fully road-legal.

Interiors

The interior of the X-Bow is also functional for racing. You won't find any heavy and unnecessary luxuries here! There's no heating, or radio, or even an instrument panel! The shells of the seats are merged into the carbon fibre body. In place of a boot, there is a detachable storage box.

Driver information such as speed and fuel level is provided via an electronic screen.

TECHNICAL INFO
Manufacturer: KTM
Car type: Racing
Engine: 2,000cc
0-60 mph: 3.9 sec

AUDI R8

The Audi R8 is an exciting and high-performance mid-engined super car. Borrowing some of its styling from Lamborghini, the R8 is a bold statement from Audi.

Did You Know?

Photographs of secret Audi testing suggest that an eagerly awaited convertible R8 is in development.

Cockpit Interior

The R8 is a 2-seater sports car with a luxurious interior. The sports seats are specially designed and finished in leather. Leather trim continues on the doors and dashboard. The R8 even comes with the option of a specially designed Bang & Olufsen sound system.

The R8 was awarded Best Handling Car of 2007 by Autocar magazine.

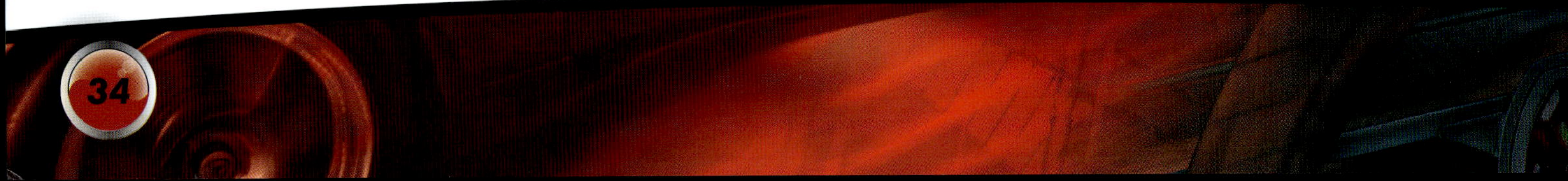

Powerful Engine

The R8 has a powerful 4.2 litre V8. Even at low speeds, the powerplant gives it a higher manoeuverability. The engine can power the car from 0-60 mph in just 4.4 seconds. The all-wheel drive system is controlled by Audi's R-tronic **gear box**. The six-speed gear box is controlled by a conventional stick-shift or by the paddles on the steering wheel. The car also has the option of **ceramic brakes**.

TECHNICAL INFO

Manufacturer: Audi
Car type: Sports
Engine: 4,163cc
0-60 mph: 4.4 sec
Top speed: 187 mph

MAGNIFICENT MACHINES

AMAZING BIKES

EXPERIENCE THE FAST LANE WITH THESE MAGNIFICENT MACHINES!

ABOUT MOTORCYCLES

A motorcycle is a two-wheeled vehicle that is powered by an engine. It can serve as an economic means of travel or can be used for sporting purposes.

Motorcycles

The first petrol-powered motorcycle was invented in 1885, when Gottlieb Daimler and Wilhelm Maybach attached an engine to a modified bicycle. As early as 1867, however, two American inventors demonstrated a 2-wheeled vehicle powered by steam propulsion. The first motorcycle available to buy went on the market in 1894 and the rest, as they say, is history!

Many Types

There are many different types of motorcycle: touring bikes are heavy and suitable for long distance travel, being designed to carry heavy luggage; sports bikes are lightweight and fast, usually with aerodynamic bodywork; off-road bikes come with big suspension forks and shock absorbers and usually have large rugged tyres for grip; cruisers are bulky motorcycles with a riding position that places the feet forward and the hands raised, tilting the rider back slightly for a more comfortable ride over long distances.

 Motorcycle designs are becoming ever more hi-tech.

Their Popularity

Generally speaking, people choose bikes because they are an economic and convenient means of transport. They usually cost less than a car, use less fuel, are quicker through traffic and are easier to park. Motorcycles, these days, are extremely popular. Around the world, various motorcycle clubs have formed. These clubs go for road trips and enjoy various activities together on their bikes.

 Cruisers are recognized for their long and low design.

DUCATI 1098R

The Ducati 1098R is the ultimate super bike. The lightest, most technologically advanced, and most powerful two-cylinder motorcycle ever built. The R stands for race bike.

 The Supertest World Association (SWA) awarded the 1098R the "*Best Bike of the Year*" in 2008.

Road-legal Race Bike

Ducati claim that the 1098R is as close to the race bike as they have ever produced. It generates 180 horsepower and weighs 165 kg (364 lbs). The 0-60 mph time is less than 2.5 seconds and top speed is 186 mph. The bike has distinctive design features such as a high tail section, compact front end, along with a non-integrated exhaust system. Superior components and advanced electronics deliver a high level of performance.

The Ducati 1098R has the highest torque-to-weight ratio of any sports bike.

The Engine

The aim of the engine designers was to create an ultra-compact engine that was more efficient and more powerful than previous engines for the next generation of Ducati super bikes. To keep the engine light but still strong, the designers used titanium, magnesium alloy and carbon fibre. The engine produces an amazing 180 horsepower. The engine has a unique 'W' shape, created by its twin-cylinder formation. A six gear transmission allows the bike to take full advantage of the speed produced.

The Body

The 1098R has the soul of a race bike. The riding position is such that man and machine become one. The basic frame weighs just 9 kg (19.8 lbs). The bike has a highly **aerodynamic** shape. The bike is fitted with an array of electronic equipment to enhance bike control.

The Testastretta Evoluzione engine on the 1098R is the lightest Ducati super bike engine ever.

TECHNICAL INFO
Class: Sport
Engine: V-Twin
Power: 180 hp @ 9,750 rpm (revolutions per minute)

The 1098R carries trademark Ducati features like the high tail section, compact front-end and twin under-seat silencers.

DUCATI SUPERBIKE 749

The Ducati Superbike 749 is the perfect super bike entry model and ideal for riders looking to experience their first thrill of riding a high-performance machine.

The Bike

The Ducati Superbike 749 incorporates many features from the 999 model. The L-twin Testastretta engine is very compact, making the finished motorcycle narrow and agile, much like its racing cousin. The 748 cc Testastretta engine supplies 108 hp. It has a smaller rear tyre, an adjustable rake and five-position adjustable rearset mounts.

- A digital display occupies centre place on the dashboard of the 749.

- Ducati reduced the size of the 749's rear tyre to improve performance.

TECHNICAL INFO
Class: Superbike
Engine: L-twin
Power: 107 hp @ 10,000 rpm
Weight: 188 kgs

The Features

The 749 is powered by a Ducati Testastretta engine. The bike has features that are the result of decades of research and development. These include advanced electronics, state-of-the-art **ergonomics** and the best aerodynamics in its class. The front suspension guarantees better stability and, consequently, better bike control.

At the heart of the 749 is the powerful Testastretta engine.

The Look

The Ducati 749's tubular trellis frame is designed for the racetrack. The suspension, both front and rear, is adjustable, resulting in a smooth ride. The Ducati 749 has two versions: regular and the new 749 Dark. The 749 Dark is the more accessible of the two, perhaps because of its darker and more stylish look. The 749 is a perfect model for the first-time rider who wants to experience the thrill of riding a Ducati.

The 749 is perfect for people who are riding a superbike for the first time.

DUCATI 999S

The Ducati 999S is a combination of power, style and comfort. It is designed for riders of all sizes and is a user-friendly performance bike.

The Race Bike

The Ducati 999S is an exciting sports bike. Long and narrow with a sleek look, the 999S showcases Ducati's experience gained over years of success at the highest levels of racing. Designed by Pierre Terblanche, it is known as an extremely high-performance, race-ready motorcycle. The 999S is at the top of its class thanks to its engine performance and outstanding weight distribution.

TECHNICAL INFO

Class: Sport
Engine: L-twin
Power: 143 hp @ 9,750 rpm
Weight: 186 kgs

The 749's outstanding weight distribution made for one of the best-handling motorcycles ever seen.

The Testastretta

The 999S features an especially powerful **Testastretta** engine that delivers 143 hp. This engine has been tried and tested on the racetrack, and is designed to give maximum output even when the the bike is accelerating or cornering. The engine has been designed with the most experienced riders in mind, who expect the best in terms of technology and performance. All in all the Testastretta engine offers the bike higher power, better performance, and greater reliability.

The 999S's engine is built to the highest levels of performance.

Other Features

The motorcycle has an adjustable riding position that provides the rider comfort and control on the road as well as the racetrack: the position of the footpegs, rake, **suspension**, plus seat/tank combination on the single-seat version, are all modifiable. The bulky front end ensures precise control and is designed to reduce pressure on the rider's wrists. A wider steering angle makes the motorcycle easy to ride in the streets.

The 999S can be set up for optimum ride quality on road or track.

HONDA CBR1000RR

The Honda CBR1000RR is a bike designed to burn up the racetrack! On its release in 2004, the bike was noted for a number of new technological elements unseen on a motorcycle before.

TECHNICAL INFO
Class: Sport
Engine: In-line four
Power: 178 hp @ 12,000 rpm
Weight: 176 kgs

Racing-Meets-Super Bike

The Honda CBR1000RR merges racing technology into a super bike and is an excellent ride on the track as well as the streets. With a comparatively lighter engine and chassis compared to other similarly-sized motorcycles, it is able to deliver more power to the wheels and makes for extreme performance.

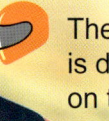

The Honda CBR1000RR is designed to perform on the racetrack.

The Powerplant

Perhaps the best feature of this motorcycle is the liquid-cooled 998 cc four-stroke engine. The engine was designed specifically with an eye toward handling as well as **horsepower**. Special attention was given to ensuring the powerplant remained an extremely compact package. This compact engine was then positioned further forward on the bike's **chassis** for an improved weight distribution.

Enviable Features

The Honda CBR1000RR comes with a high-capacity 350-watt AC generator. The LED taillights and folding aerodynamic mirrors embellish the appearance. There is a plastic tank shell cover that protects the airbox and the tank. A one-piece fan assembly efficiently cools the engine and there is an ignition switch/**fork** lock for greater security. To improve the handling, Honda engineers also lightened as many pieces as possible.

The four cylinder engine is the most outstanding feature of the CBR1000RR.

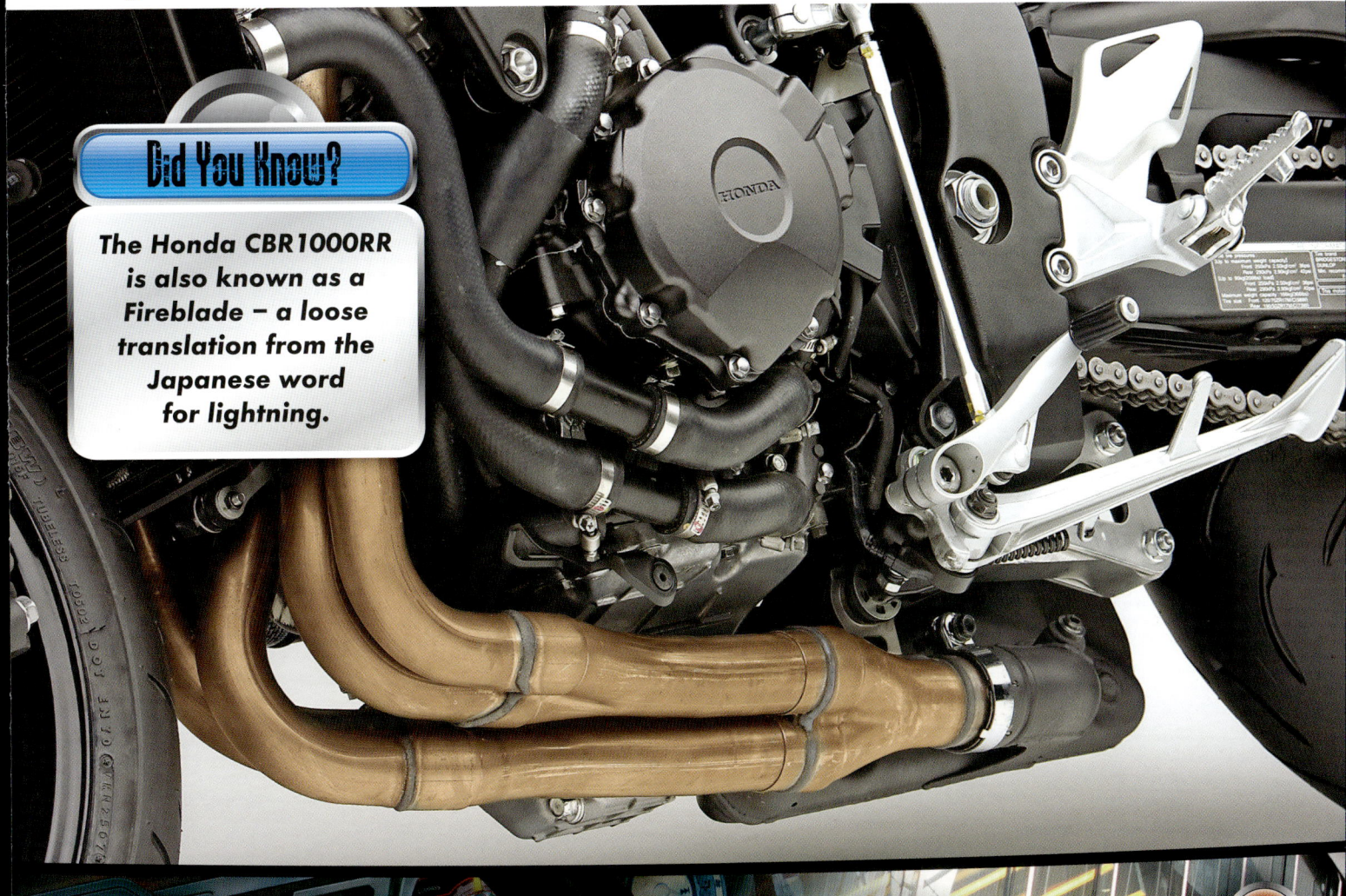

Did You Know?

The Honda CBR1000RR is also known as a Fireblade – a loose translation from the Japanese word for lightning.

HONDA SHADOW SPIRIT 750 C2

The Honda Shadow Spirit 750 C2 is one of Honda's finest cruising motorcycles. Easy to manoeuvre, this motorcycle is a combination of power and style.

Long and low, the Shadow Spirit is a landmark Honda bike.

Long and Low

The Shadow Spirit 750 C2 is a long motorcycle, with a low-slung seat similar to larger-engined heavyweight cruisers. The user-friendly ergonomics and handling comfort makes it a good motorcycle for first-time riders. The single backbone frame of the motorcycle gives it a longer wheelbase, and the stretched shape accommodates physically larger riders. Fortunately, the seat is only 25.7 inches from the ground, so most riders find the bike accommodating.

TECHNICAL INFO

Class: Cruiser
Engine: In-line four
Power: 131 bhp @ 14,000 rpm
Weight: 228 kg

Oodles of Attitude

Every element of the Shadow Spirit's design shrieks out attitude. The new handlebar offers a sporty, upright riding position. The low scooped-out seat and a teardrop-shaped air cleaner cover add to the hot-rod aura. Other signature elements of the Shadow Spirit include the rear fender, with a custom, integrated taillight, a chromed, tank-mounted instrument panel and twin, bullet-style mufflers.

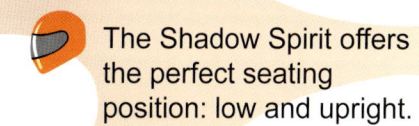

The Shadow Spirit offers the perfect seating position: low and upright.

Easy Handling

Despite its weight (228 kg), the Honda Spirit 750 C2 is relatively easy to **manoeuvre** for a bike of its size. Similarly, the larger and narrower front wheel makes for light and agile handling when cruising over distance.

With its easy manoeuverability, the bike has become a very popular cruiser.

KAWASAKI NINJA ZX-10R

The Ninja ZX-10R is a high-performance sports bike, hailed as the best super bike in the world upon its release.

Technology

The Kawasaki Ninja ZX-10R was designed for the racetrack. It has an advanced chassis technology and greater horsepower than other open-class supersport motorcycles. It seems that the engineers have also kept in mind the street riders while designing this motorcycle, demonstrated by the stability and the ease of handling.

The Kawasaki Ninja ZX-10R is designed for the racetrack but can be ridden on the streets as well.

Did You Know?

The Kawasaki Ninja ZX-10R is capable of going from 0-60 mph in just 2.9 seconds.

Highlights

This racing monster is powered by a 998 cc high-performance engine. The wheels feature a new six spoke design that are as light as racing wheels. Street riders will appreciate the bike's solid stability and predictable handling. The Kawasaki Ninja ZX-10R has an efficient **exhaust** system that not only flows better than the ZX-9R but gives off less noise and emissions as well.

Power all the Way

The ZX-10R is designed for the racing enthusiast. The bike is built for the accomplished rider who can fully appreciate its capabilities. Whether put to the test at a racetrack, or merely the focus of racing conversation, the bike is, by all standards, the embodiment of the ultimate super bike.

The ZX-10R has a very efficient exhaust system that keeps noise and emissions to a minimum.

TECHNICAL INFO
Class: Sport
Engine: In-line four
Weight: 175 kgs

KAWASAKI VULCAN 900 CUSTOM

The Kawasaki Vulcan 900 Custom has great looks, is powerful, and comes with features that are uniquely different from other bikes.

Looks

The Kawasaki Vulcan 900 Custom has the power and feel of a bigger motorcycle. It is designed to stand out from the rest. The sleek bodywork, the big rear tyre and the slender-looking front end makes this motorcycle a true eye catcher.

Features

Kawasaki's engineers have delivered a motorcycle that provides the customized appearance you'd expect from an expensive, exclusive motorcyle. The combination of the low rear end and the slender front end is perfect. But it is not just pretty looking. The V-Twin engine gives it the necessary **torque** and power.

The Kawasaki Vulcan 900 Custom has everything: great looks and great power.

The Custom Bike

The Vulcan 900 Custom's contrasting front and rear end is completemented by the teardrop-shaped fuel tank. The sculpted bodywork of the bike add to the custom feel, which is topped off by the slim, oversized, 21 inch front wheel, with specially designed spokes.

Did You Know?

The Kawasaki Vulcan 900 Custom comes in three colours: Metallic Diablo Black, Passion Red and Candy Lime Green.

The Kawasaki Vulcan 900 Custom is a mean machine for a mid-sized cruiser.

TECHNICAL INFO

Class: Custom Cruiser
Engine: 903 cc, V-twin, 4-stroke
Weight: 249 kgs

BMW K1200LT

The BMW K1200LT is a large touring bike. It is easy to handle and engineered for comfort over long stretches of road.

Touring in Style

The BMW K1200LT is a touring motorcycle with many excellent features. A high-output powerplant, an advanced gearbox, chrome package, and an electro-hydraulic centre stand, make this motorcycle among the most comfortable imaginable. An advanced damper system on the suspension helps smooth out the bumps and keep the bike stable over long distances.

The BMW K1200LT is designed for long distance touring.

Did You Know?

The BMW K1200LT even has lights that illuminate the ground for mounting and dismounting the bike at night!

Cruising Along

The K1200LT is powered by a water-cooled 1,173 cc engine that generates about 100 horsepower. The bike comes with a 60 ampere alternator that puts out 840 watts of electrical power – so you can run a lot of electrical gadgets while on the road. The bike handles well both on long-distance touring and all-round riding. The six-speed gearbox allows the rider easy acceleration or deceleration, and an overall smooth ride.

A Bike With Everything

The K1200LT has an on-board computer that tells you the temperature, average speed, and fuel consumption. The bike's console features a vast array of lights, buttons and indicators. There is ample storage space for luggage, an on-board entertainment system and even heated handle grips and seats for those cold days!

Perhaps the best feature of the K1200LT is its on-board computer.

BMW CRUISER R 1200 C MONTAUK

The BMW Cruiser R 1200 C Montauk is the latest evolution of BMW's unique cruiser class. This bike has been manufactured with cutting-edge design and is smooth and comfortable to ride, as well as being extremely reliable.

The Cruiser

The Montauk is not a super bike; at least not in the racing sense. The motorcycle is at its best when it is in cruise mode at average revs. It is more tough-looking than other cruisers, which was the objective of the engineers when they got down to designing this cruiser. All in all, it one of BMW's most stylish bikes, with good power and reliable drivetrain and brakes.

The Montauk is a tough-looking cruiser.

Everything You Need...

The 1,170 cc powerplant generates 61 horsepower. The Montauk gets its own wide handlebar, Telelever fork, front fender, small windshield and unique stacked dual headlights with a larger beam over a smaller one. The seat is more sculpted with a small passenger pad. The bike comes with heated grips, a tachometer, and a clock.

... With Excellent Handling

The Montauk rides much smoother than some other BMW cruisers. The riding position is comfortable and the short windshield offers some wind protection. The front wheel is bulky, but the wide handlebar and the reduced weight of the cruiser allow the motorcycle to turn well, even under breaking.

Did You Know?

The BMW R 1200 C Montauk has even featured in a James Bond movie.

BMW K1200S

The BMW K1200S is a super bike in the truest sense of the word. Contemporary looking, it is a powerful machine as well.

The Technology

The BMW K1200S is an engineering masterpiece, with a combination of high-end technology, design and performance. The motorcycle can accelerate from 0-60 mph in less than 3 seconds. The K1200S is performance personified.

The K1200S is contemporary in design and powerful as well.

The Powerplant

The compact, liquid-cooled, four-cylinder powerplant is set across the frame instead of along. The engine bank, the main part of the engine, is angled forwards at 55 degrees, improving the steering and front wheel traction – a prerequisite for a powerful motorcycle like the BMW K1200S. But its most outstanding feature is its full electronic controls for dampers and springs.

A Thrilling Ride

The chassis of the BMW K1200S reacts well under all conditions, with good response and feedback from the front wheel. A radical suspension, innovative technologies and advanced brakes make this bike a thrilling ride.

🪖 The rear of the bike contains a small

TECHNICAL INFO
Class: Sport
Engine: In-line four
Power: 167 hp
@ 10,250 rpm
Weight: 227 kg

BMW R1200R

The compact BMW R1200R is a powerful machine. Do not be fooled by its sleek looks; this is a versatile and genuine all-rounder.

A Bike with Attitude

The BMW R1200R is all about attitude. A motorcycle capable of exhilarating performance, the R1200R has the horsepower and acceleration to satisfy the adrenaline junkie. It has the latest version of BMW's Integral Anti-lock Braking System and an Automatic Stability Control System. The motorcycle is indeed exciting.

Every aspect of the R1200R has attitude.

Sleek and Light

The R1200R's 1,170 cc engine generates 109 hp, with an oil-cooler fitted behind the wheel fork. The rear section of the motorcycle's frame has been specially constructed, giving the motorcycle a sleek appearance and reducing its overall weight.

Did You Know?

The BMW R1200R's average fuel consumption is 50 miles per gallon.

The 1,170 cc engine of the R1200R pumps out ample power.

Understated Body

The compact-looking R1200R has noticeably understated body components. This is purposefully done to highlight the technical features of the machine, and of the engine in particular. The headlight is contemporary, with free-form reflectors integrated in to the rest of the motorcycle's body, creating a tough-looking front end.

BMW R1150RS

The BMW R1150RS is a touring motorcycle with most of the attributes a rider looks for: reliability, decent speed and comfort.

Not for Racing

The BMW R1150RS is not designed for speed, but rather is designed for comfort, stability and smooth riding over long distances. Though not as glamorous as the other motorcycles in the BMW cruiser class, this tourer is highly user-friendly.

Did You Know?

RT stands for Reise-Tourer, or Travel Tourer. BMW launched their first RT in the late 1970's.

The BMW R1150RS is designed for long journeys.

Long Distance Runner

The four-valve, 1,130 cc twin engine features six-speed transmission. The big screen provides protection from wind and harsh weather. The throttle is smooth and responsive. This tourer is not the fastest on two wheels, but with a top speed of 134 mph, it gives the rider enough to get excited about.

A Comfortable Ride

The riding position is comfortable. The handle bars even come with heated grips for use in cold weather! The screen and handlebars are adjustable, as is the wide and well-padded seat, which is important on such a big, heavy bike weighing 246 kgs.

TECHNICAL INFO

Class: Touring
Engine: Two-cylinder boxer
Power: 95 hp @ 7,500 rpm
Weight: 246 kg

The big boxer engine of the R1150RS provides lots of acceleration.

BIG DOG K-9

This dog is truly big! At nine feet long, it can be a bit of a handful for some riders. The pared down design is a combination of tough and sleek. One thing's for sure: the K-9 is a motorcycle that will turn heads!

Did You Know?

The Big Dog K-9 has a 300mm-wide rear tyre!

The Really Big Dog

The K-9 is one of the best chopper models to come from Big Dog, a famous name in custom motorcycles. It is a really BIG bike, with a length of 108 inches (9 feet). For a bike of its size, the K-9 offers surprising ease of handling and control, and awesome power.

The Big Dog K-9 stands out from the crowd.

Monster Features

The K-9 weighs close to 330 kilograms and, as with most custom bikes from the Big Dog stable, has a distinctively fat rear tyre. the 39 degree front rake (angle from the handlebars to the front wheel) combines with the narrow tank to exaggerate the length. Other features include billet wheels, a 2-into-1 exhaust, and two-piece rotors. The braking is delivered by the four-piston billet calibers.

Monster Looks

This monster bike also comes with an A-frame swingarm suspension that makes riding over long distances and rough terrain a surprisingly comfortable experience. All in all, the K-9 looks the part of a custom bike – cool and heavily styled, with stripped-back bodywork and oversized front forks.

TECHNICAL INFO
Class: Chopper
Engine: V-twin
Weight: 328 kgs

The Big Dog K-9 stays functional and eye-catching at the same time.

MTT TURBINE

This is the most powerful bike in the world! It's also one of the longest and, not to mention, most visually striking!

Turbine Engine

The MTT Turbine is only the world's second wheel driven motorcycle powered by a turbine engine. The engine is mounted upside down on a custom aluminium frame. The MTT is powered by a converted Rolls Royce Allison 250 series turboshaft engine that is capable of producing up to 320 hp!

Beauty Meets Technology

The body is made of lightweight carbon fibre panels. There are two slash-cut exhausts that disperse the heat. The motorcycle also represents the latest in cutting-edge technology, featuring carbon fibre fairings, rear mounted camera equipped with an LCD colour display, a radar detector with laser scrambler, a one touch "Smart Start" ignition, and much more.

The MTT Turbine is driven by a turbine engine that has been converted and re-built.

Did You Know?

The MTT Turbine is to be replaced by the MTT Streetfighter in 2008, another jet-powered bike with even more power!

These converted turbine engines start life on aircraft such as helicopters.

The Beast

The motorcycle has a reported top speed of 227 mph and comes with a hefty price tag – a cool $150,000US! Indeed, when it was launched it was recognised by Guinness World Records as the most powerful and most expensive production motorcycle in the world. Riding this machine is believed to be quite a handful due to the sudden acceleration and its long body.

DIGGERS, TRUCKS & EARTH MOVERS

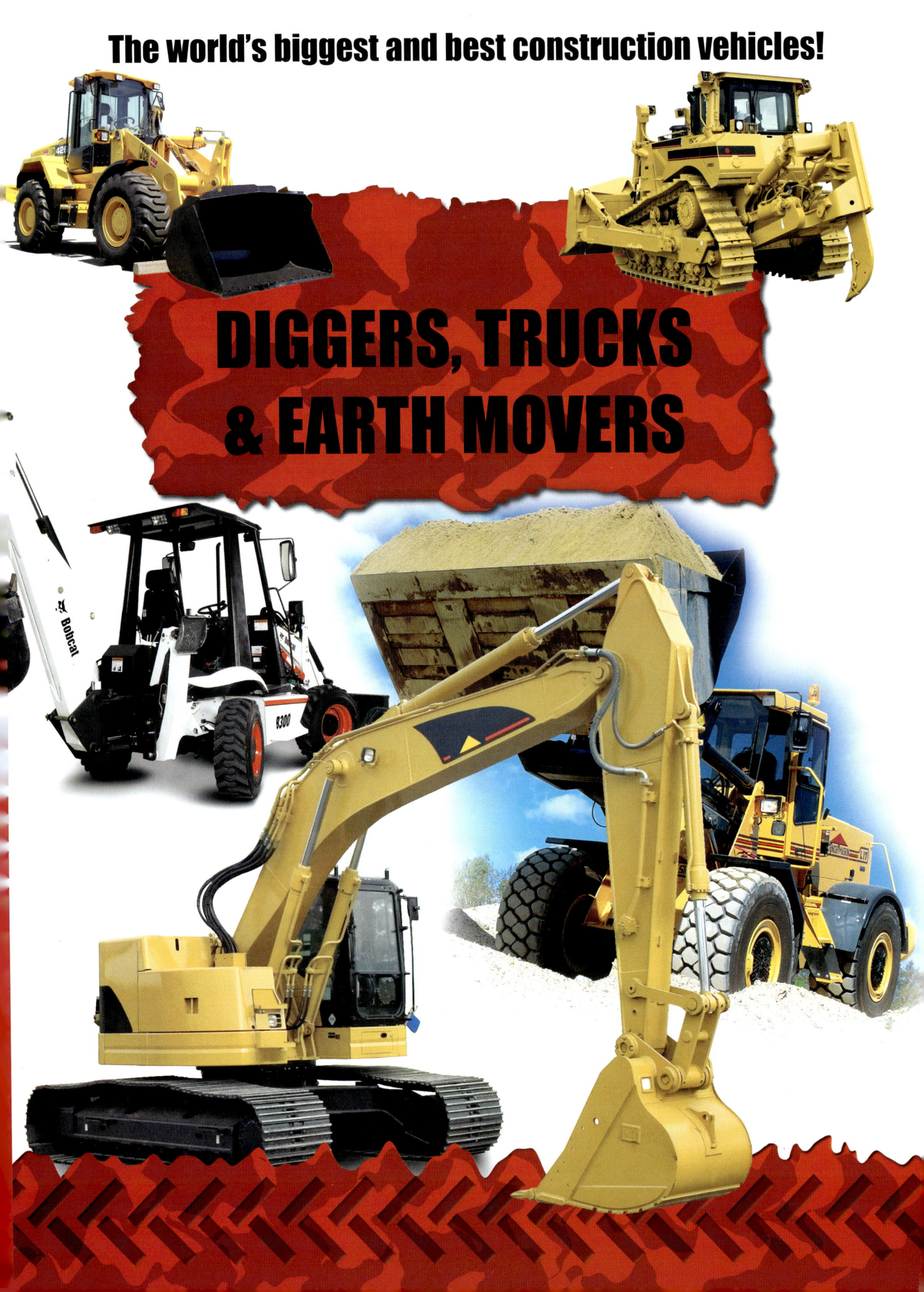

The world's biggest and best construction vehicles!

HYDRAULICS AT WORK

Have you wondered how huge vehicles like diggers and cranes are able to work so swiftly and efficiently? These huge machines require a lot of power to perform heavy-duty tasks. The principle behind the working of these vehicles is known as hydraulics.

How it works

Imagine two cylinders containing oil, connected by a narrow pipe, as shown in the picture. When the first cylinder is pushed down, the level of oil in the second cylinder rises because the force applied on the first cylinder is multiplied and transmitted to the second cylinder through the pipe. This is the basic principle used in all hydraulic machinery.

▸ The simple diagram (right) depicts the principle of hydraulics

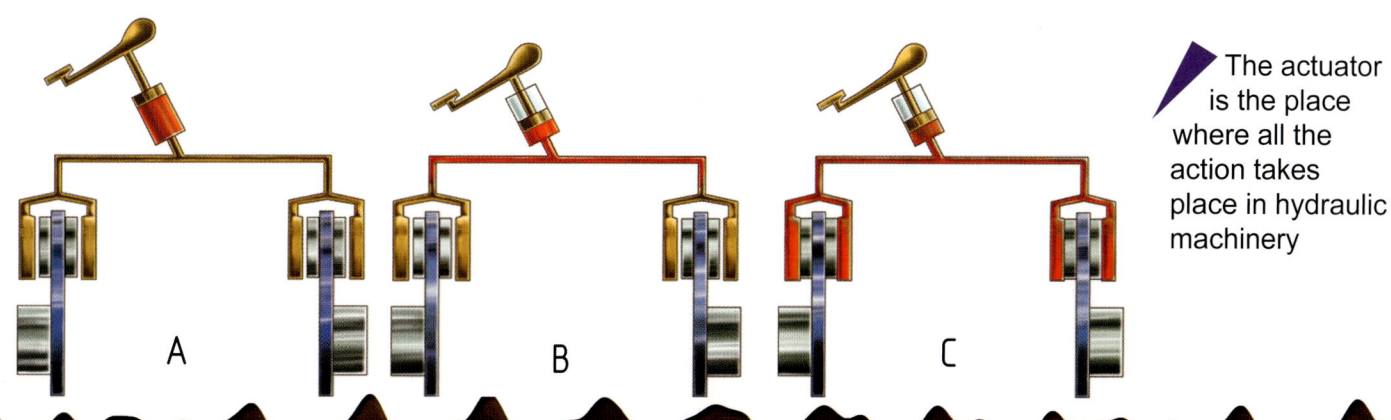

Basic parts

Any hydraulic machinery will consist of several essential parts. One is a hydraulic pump that pushes the oil into the system. The pump is connected to an engine through gears or belts. Any hydraulic machinery also has an actuator, which is the point where all the action takes place. In the case of a digger, it is the hydraulic cylinder. A control valve helps to direct the fluid into the desired actuator. The oil that is pushed into the cylinder flows back into the pump or, in some cases, a reservoir, where it is filtered for re-use.

▸ The actuator is the place where all the action takes place in hydraulic machinery

67

BULLDOZERS

The bulldozer is one of the most common construction vehicles. It is a huge tractor fitted with a dozer blade – a large, curved metal plate. Bulldozers are used to remove huge obstacles and remains of structures.

Early bulldozers

Early bulldozers were simply modified farm tractors. They had a huge metal plate to move layers of soil and their success prompted companies to make proper bulldozers. They were named bulldozers because they were noisy and powerful.

▶ The blades of early bulldozers were not curved as they are now

Tracked for success

Imagine driving a large tractor over piles of debris, and moving huge boulders and tons of metal out of the way! Bulldozers are equipped with special parts. Instead of wheels, they have huge metal belts called tracks. The tracks help to distribute the vehicle weight over a larger area, enabling it to move on all types of surface.

▶ The tracks enable the bulldozer to move on sandy and muddy surfaces

DIGGERS, TRUCKS & EARTH MOVERS

Modern bulldozers have rippers that can break the hardest boulders into pieces

Mean machine

Modern bulldozers use different types of blades depending upon the work that is to be done. The straight blade (or s-blade) is short and thick, and is used for fine grading. The universal blade (u-blade) is tall and curved. It has large side wings to carry more materials. A combination blade is slightly curved and has smaller side wings. Some bulldozers have huge claw-like equipment at the back, known as a ripper.

SUPER DOZER

The Komatsu D575 is the largest bulldozer in the world. Built by a Japanese company named Komatsu, this bulldozer is used in coal mining. The monstrous vehicle is 4.88 m (16 feet) tall and 11.72 m (38.5 feet) long! Its blade is almost 7.5 m (25 feet) wide.

69

LOADERS

Loaders are wheeled tractors that have a huge, rectangular bucket in the front to lift and move material. The bucket can be replaced with a mechanical claw-like device to carry loads.

A loader by any name

There are several different types of loaders, such as front, backhoe and skid loaders. Front loaders are usually large with a front bucket mainly used for loading sand and dirt on to trucks and clearing rubble. Sometimes, front loaders are also used for digging. However, they do not make good diggers, as they cannot dig very deep below their wheels.

Loaders can also lift their buckets high up to carry materials short distances

Like in the front loader, the bucket of a skid loader can also be replaced with a snowplough attachment, backhoe or even a concrete pump

Skid loaders

Loaders with fixed tyres that do not turn are called skid loaders. To change direction, the driver changes the spinning speed between the left and right tyres. Skid loaders are smaller and lighter than front loaders but are similar in that they have a wide bucket at the front.

Backhoe loaders

Hydraulic

Backhoe loaders are so called because they have a digging arm at the back, as well as a front bucket. The backhoe can be permanent or removable. Backhoe loaders are more efficient at digging than front loaders and are extensively used for this purpose. They are also used to demolish small structures, transport building materials over short distances and to break asphalt and paved roads. The front bucket sometimes has a detachable bottom that enables the vehicle to empty its load.

DIGGERS, TRUCKS & EARTH MOVERS

Loaders with permanent backhoes have a swivel seat that can turn around to face the backhoe controls

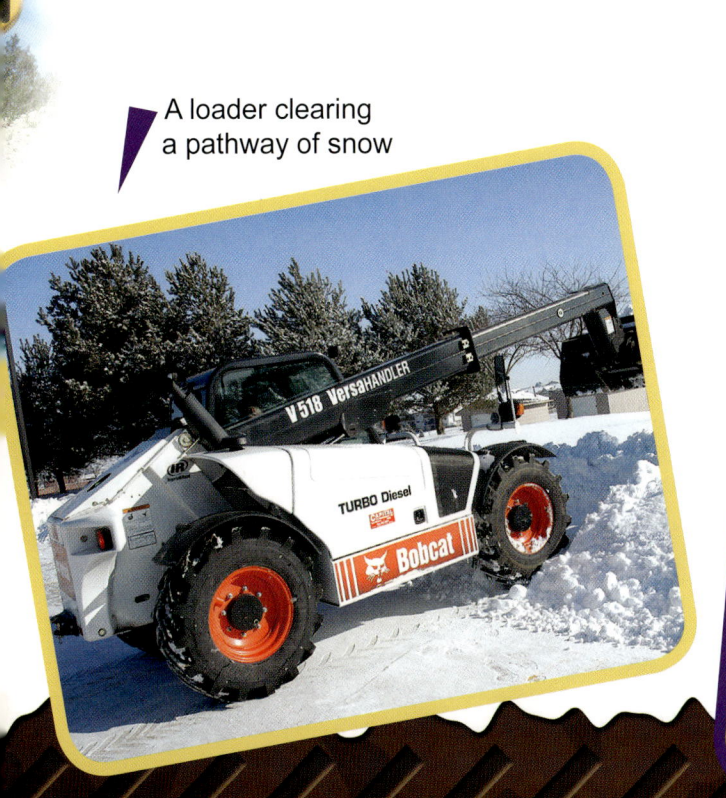

A loader clearing a pathway of snow

PLOUGHING THROUGH SNOW

During winters, loaders are used to remove snow after heavy snowfalls. Skid loaders are especially good for the job, since they are light and can be manoeuvred easily. Special loaders mill the surface of the road with their rough roller attachment, making the road less slippery and safer for vehicles.

DIGGERS

Diggers, or excavators, are used primarily for digging large holes and foundations. They are also used for demolition, heavy-lifting and mining. Diggers have a backhoe and a cab that can rotate on its wheels or tracks.

Types of diggers

There are many varieties of diggers. Some are small and are known as mini or compact diggers. Micro-shovels are diggers that are the size of a motorcycle. They are used to dig and level ground in small, inaccessible places like narrow lanes. Most compact diggers have a small blade attached to the undercarriage that is used for pushing debris away.

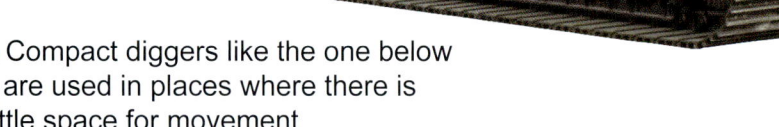

Boom

Driver's

The backhoe or bucket of a digger can be replaced with other devices like grapplers or breakers

Compact diggers like the one below are used in places where there is little space for movement

Digging deeper

Diggers can be used to dig out mud and silt from sea and riverbeds. This process is called dredging. Dredging is a technique also used when creating new harbours, deepening ports, removing rubbish from sea and river beds and obtaining fresh sand for beaches.

Dredgers

There are many kinds of dredgers. Some dredging jobs require large scale equipment. Large land diggers with specialised crawlers are used to dig sand from riverbeds. The crawler prevents the digger from sinking. Dredging pipes, connected to ships, are often used to suck in silt from the bottom of seas and rivers. Land diggers can also be mounted on pontoons, or barges, for the same purpose. Submersibles with caterpillar tracks, which crawl on the seabed, are used to dig and recover material from the seabed.

MIGHTY DREDGER

The W. D. Fairway is the world's largest dredger. This 173 m-long ship is a suction hopper dredger with a hold called a hopper onboard. The silt that is dredged is dropped into this hopper. Once the hopper is full, the dredger returns to the dumpsite, where the bottom doors of the hopper are opened to empty the silt out.

The term 'dredger' refers not only to land diggers, but also to ships and submersibles that carry out dredging in deeper waters. Dredging ships and submersibles are often used to level the seabed and lay underwater cables

DIGGERS, TRUCKS & EARTH MOVERS

DRAGLINES

Dragline excavators are diggers that are mainly used in strip-mining operations to extract coal and other minerals. Smaller draglines are also used for constructing roads and ports. Draglines are some of the largest vehicles.

Parts of a dragline

A dragline excavator comprises a hoist rope, hoist coupler, dragline bucket, drag coupler and drag rope. Draglines used in mining can move up to 450,000 kg (992,080 pounds) of material at a time! Dragline booms are normally between 45-100 m (148-328 ft) in length. Most draglines do not have wheels or caterpillar tracks. They move by 'walking' with the help of pontoons.

The main difference between draglines and other mining equipment is that the former are not powered by fuel, but electricity. They are usually connected directly to high-voltage grids

Dragline in action

DIGGERS, TRUCKS & EARTH MOVERS

Operating a dragline

Unlike other diggers, draglines do not use hydraulics. The bucket is operated with a hoist and drag ropes. The hoist rope is used to lower and lift the bucket. The bucket is drawn along the surface using the drag rope. The bucket is then swung around to the dumping ground and the drag rope released to tilt the bucket and dump the material.

▶ The mining dragline can drill and deliver well crushed rock to the excavating and loading equipment

Big Muskie

Big Muskie, the largest single-bucket digger in the world was built by Bucyrus-Erie of the United States. This coal-mining dragline was owned by the Central Ohio Coal Company and was as tall as a 22-storey building. It was used in coalmines in Ohio, U.S. for about 22 years and finally dismantled in 1999. The most amazing feature of the dragline - a bucket that could hold more than 10 cars - has been preserved.

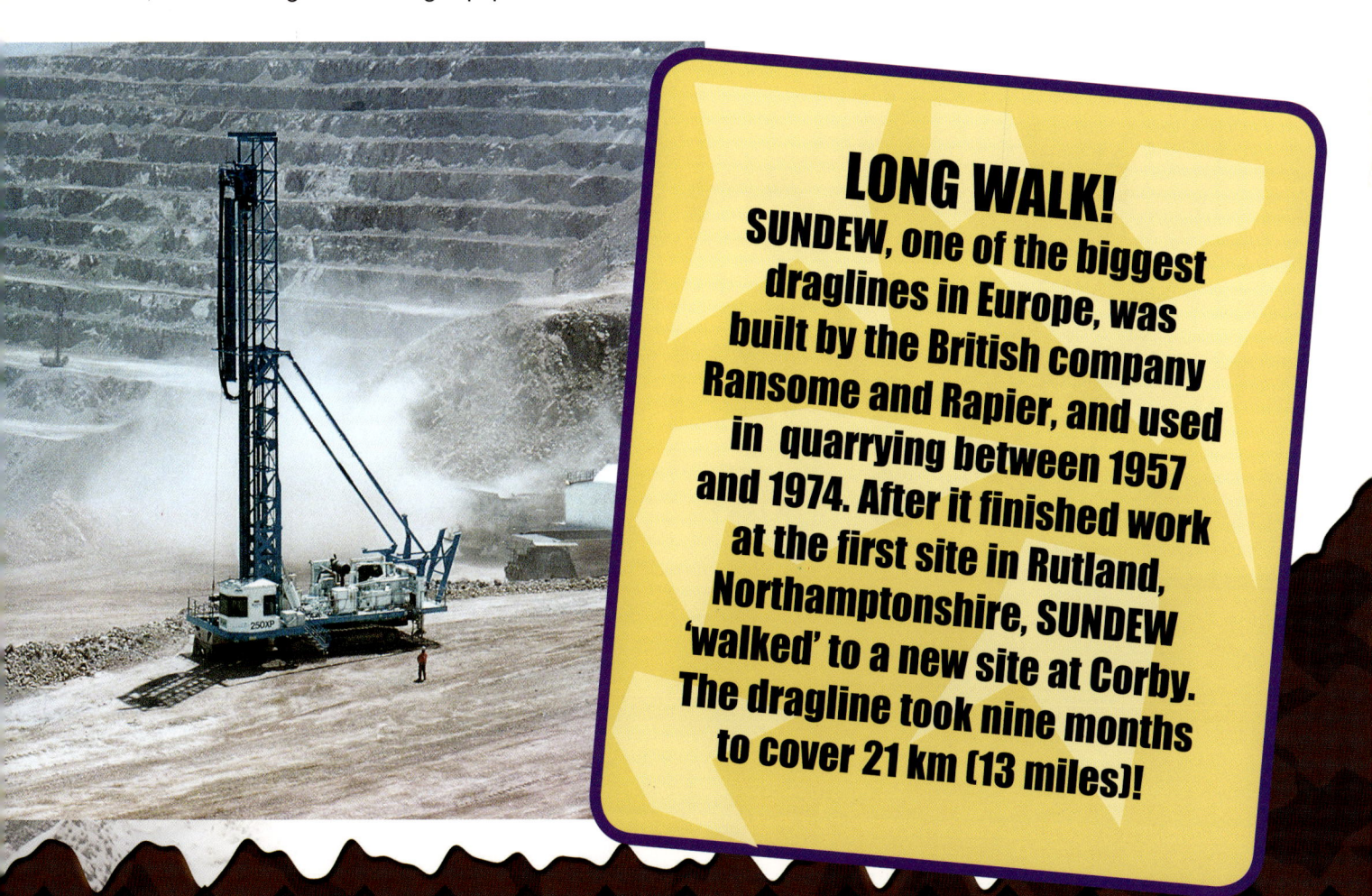

LONG WALK!

SUNDEW, one of the biggest draglines in Europe, was built by the British company Ransome and Rapier, and used in quarrying between 1957 and 1974. After it finished work at the first site in Rutland, Northamptonshire, SUNDEW 'walked' to a new site at Corby. The dragline took nine months to cover 21 km (13 miles)!

CRANES

Cranes lift and lower heavy loads. Often seen at construction sites, they are usually stationed temporarily at the site. Cranes can be fixed to the ground or transported to the site whenever they are required.

Cranes from the past

While not as large or varied as modern cranes, cranes of the past played an important role in construction. Cranes were used during the Middle Ages to build castles and cathedrals and to load ships in ports. Some medieval cranes had to be fixed on top of the wall that was being constructed while workers ran large wheels on either side to power the crane.

▸ Medieval cranes, like the one in the picture below, were usually made of wood

▸ Cranes come in various sizes and forms. Their functions also differ greatly, but all cranes consist of a jib and a lifting cable

Jib

Counterweight

Crane parts

Every crane stands on a supporting base and rotates using a slewing unit or motor. The jib, an extension of the boom, is the arm of the crane that lifts the load. A trolley runs along the jib to help move the load. Cranes are usually operated from the cab but some have a push-button control station at the base, while others can be operated from a remote station using infrared or radio signals.

DIGGERS, TRUCKS & EARTH MOVERS

▸ Cranes can lift extremely heavy loads including large shipping containers and vehicles

Working a hydraulic crane

The commonly used crane comprises two-gear pumps to pressurise the oil. When pressure increases, the oil flows into cylinders operating the boom of the crane and helps it move up. Releasing pressure brings the boom down. Several cable lines run down the entire length of the boom and jib and are connected to a metal ball that pulls them tight when not carrying loads. A gear under the operator's cab helps to turn the boom around. This is controlled using hydraulic foot-pedals in the cab. Outriggers and counterweights help to balance the crane.

A MONUMENTAL TASK

The Egyptian obelisk at St. Peter's Square in the Vatican was transported to the Square in 1586 by Domenico Fontana, an Italian architect. It took about 40 winches, 75 horses, a huge wooden tower and almost a thousand men to lift the obelisk and stand it upright in the Square.

CRANE MANIA

The most common types of cranes are mobile, telescopic, tower, gantry, stacker and floating cranes. Gantry and stacker cranes are not used for construction but, instead, are used in manufacturing and in ports for loading and unloading.

Mobile cranes

The most basic cranes are mobile cranes, comprising a boom mounted on a mobile carrier such as a truck or caterpillar tracks. The boom of the crane can be raised and lowered on hinges at the bottom, using cables and pulleys or even hydraulic cylinders, as in the case of hydraulic truck cranes. A hook suspended from the top of the boom is attached to cables that run through the length of the boom. Mobile cranes can be used for demolition by attaching a huge metal ball to the hook, or converted into a digger by adding a bucket or dragline to the boom.

Tower cranes

Tower cranes are used in the construction of tall buildings. Fixed to the ground and taller than the structure that is to be built, tower cranes comprise a vertical tower and a horizontal boom. The long arm of the boom carries the load, while the short arm carries concrete blocks as counterweights. A tower crane is often assembled using a telescopic crane, which comprises a boom divided into many tubes placed one inside another and can be extended or retracted hydraulically.

▼ A crawler crane is mounted on an undercarriage with caterpillar tracks. A rough terrain crane has rubber tyres

DIGGERS, TRUCKS & EARTH MOVERS

Floating cranes

These are used to construct ports and bridges, load and unload ships and even to lift up sunken ships. Floating cranes are mounted on pontoons or barges. Cranes on barges are huge and can lift thousands of tonnes of load, and are preferred for building bridges.

◀ A floating crane building a bridge. Cranes like these are also used to salvage shipwrecks from the bottom of the sea

◀ Telescopic cranes can be attached to transporter vehicles to unload goods upon arrival - in this case onto the roof of a building

STANDING TALL!
The K-10, 000, the largest tower crane in the world, was built by Kroll, a Danish company. At 120 m (394 feet), the crane is nearly three times as tall as the Statue of Liberty. Its boom has a reach of about 90 m (295 feet) and can lift two Challenger tanks. It can withstand wind speeds of over 280km/hour (174 mph).

SCRAPERS

Scrapers are large earth-moving vehicles, similar to diggers and bulldozers, which are mainly used in canal and road construction. However, some scrapers can also be used in agriculture and land levelling.

The beginning

Modern scrapers are based on the revolutionary Fresno scraper, invented by Scottish businessman James Porteous in 1883. Working with farmers in Fresno, California, Porteous realised the need for a faster and more efficient way of building canals in sandy soil and this started him on the design for a new scraper. After discussions with other inventors working on similar designs, Porteous bought their patents to become Fresno Scraper's sole patent holder.

Fresno scrapers were widely used in construction works during the early 1900s. They were even used in the construction of the Panama Canal

James Porteous, the inventor of the Fresno scraper

Revolutionary design

The Fresno scraper scooped up soil instead of pushing it along the ground, like similar machines of its time. Porteous' scraper had a C-shaped bowl with a blade attached along the bottom. The scraper was pulled by horses while the operator walked behind holding its handle. Lifting the handle made the blade cut into soil and load it into the bowl. When the bowl was full, the operator lowered the handle to tilt it up. The operator could change the angle of the bowl using the handle, thereby depositing soil anywhere.

DIGGERS, TRUCKS & EARTH MOVERS

Back   Hydraulic

Vertical

A modern scraper, such as the one in the picture above, is used extensively in the construction of canals and roads

Scraper at work

Modern scrapers consist of a hopper and a tractor that moves it up and down using hydraulics. When the hopper is lowered, the front part cuts into the soil and loads it into the hopper. When full, the operator raises the hopper. A vertical blade prevents the soil from falling out. At the destination, the vertical blade is opened and the hopper's back panel pushed forward to unload the soil. Today, there are many kinds of scrapers including open bowl scrapers, tandem scrapers, elevating and auger scrapers.

TYPES OF SCRAPERS
Open bowl scrapers have a push-cat that helps to load material by pushing the scraper. Tandem scrapers have two engines. The extra power is needed in steep or slippery places. Elevating and auger scrapers are self-loading. They have a looping device that loads the material into the bowl.

81

TRUCKS

Moving heavy loads over land has been a lot easier since the invention of the wheel. Today, we use trucks of all sizes to transport building materials to and from construction sites. Trucks are even used to transport huge cranes and diggers from one site to another.

▼ Steam trucks like this one were once commonly used to transport goods from one place to another

Early trucks

Trucks came into existence after the invention of the steam engine. Until then, horse-drawn carriages were the fastest mode of transport. By the mid-1800s steam trucks, which were faster and could carry heavy loads, became popular. However, the roads of the time did not allow for long distance transport. Steam trucks were, therefore, used only to carry goods from the factory to the nearest train station or port.

Towards a brighter future

In 1898, Gottlieb Daimler built the first internal combustion engine. This new invention gave trucks more power and increased load capacity. After World War I, many more inventions such as pneumatic tyres, power brakes and six-cylinder engines came into use. This also revolutionised truck design and carrying capacity. Soon, the first modern semi-trailers made their appearance.

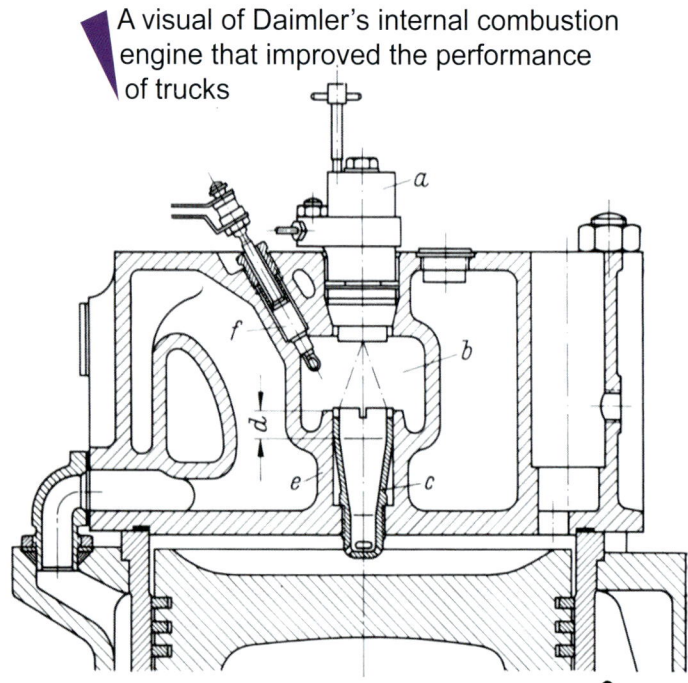

▼ A visual of Daimler's internal combustion engine that improved the performance of trucks

82

DIGGERS, TRUCKS & EARTH MOVERS

Larger trucks are often used for transporting smaller vehicles to construction sites - sometimes on specially designed trailers, as in the picture above

Parts of a truck

All modern trucks comprise a chassis, a cab, axles, wheels, suspension and an engine. The steel or aluminium chassis forms the framework of the truck to which other parts are attached. The cab is the enclosed space for the driver. Some trucks have a sleeper attached to the cab for the driver to rest in when they're not driving. Most modern trucks use diesel engines. Light trucks such as pickup trucks, however, use petrol engines.

MONSTER TRUCK

The Terex Titan is the largest tandem-axle dump truck in the world. Built by General Motors in 1974, it was used in the coalmine at Sparwood in British Columbia, Canada. The 235 ton monster truck is powered by a 16-cylinder engine. It is 20 m (66 feet) long and has a width of 7.57m (24'10"). Its tyres are about 3.35 m (11 feet) in diameter.

DUMP TRUCKS

Dump trucks are used to carry sand, gravel, rocks, bricks and other loads, to and from construction sites.

Dumping loads

A dump truck usually comprises an open box that is operated hydraulically. The outer edge of the box is attached to the back of the truck, but its inner edge can be lifted to "dump" materials at the site. Different dump trucks perform different tasks.

Trailer dump trucks

These trucks consist of a trailer that is pulled by a tractor. A semi-end dump truck has a trailer with a hydraulic hoist that tips the trailer. The bottom dump truck has the dump gate at the bottom of the trailer. The containers have sloping sides so that the material can be off-loaded through the bottom by opening the gate.

Dump box

A standard dump truck has a dump box mounted on the truck's chassis. The hydraulic ram between the cab and the dump box lifts the box when material has to be off-loaded

Hydraulic

Driver's

84

Other dump trucks

Side dump trucks are trailer dump trucks with hydraulic rams that tip the box to either side while off-loading. Dump trucks with crawlers are used on muddy and uneven sites. These trucks can be easily manoeuvred in narrow spaces by turning their upper parts around.

DIGGERS, TRUCKS & EARTH MOVERS

MONSTER DUMP TRUCKS

Off-road dump trucks are used at coal and diamond mines to carry heavy loads across uneven paths. In some mines, super large dump trucks are required for the extremely heavy payload. These vehicles can be over 45 feet long and 20 feet tall, with tyres twice as high as an adult.

Off-road dump trucks are huge and used mainly at mining sites to haul heavy dirt and rocks

MIXERS

A concrete mixer is one of the most common machines seen at any construction site. It is used to make concrete by mixing cement, sand and water. Some concrete mixers are small enough to be moved manually. Large concrete mixers mounted on trucks are used for heavy construction work.

Portable mixers

A concrete mixer consists of a drum that revolves to mix the various substances used to make concrete. Small portable mixers have wheels that help to move them around. The drum is rotated using electricity. Cement, sand and water are poured in to the drum manually. Once the concrete is mixed thoroughly, the drum is tilted to pour the mixture out.

Mixer trucks

Truck-mounted concrete mixers are one of the most widely used construction vehicles. They consist of a large revolving drum that is filled with ready-to-mix concrete at the factory. As the truck is driven to the construction site, the drum keeps revolving in order to prevent the concrete from hardening.

A truck-mounted concrete mixer dumping concrete at the site

A portable concrete mixer at a construction site

The design of modern screw pumps, used to pump sewage in sewage treatment plants, is based on the principle of the Archimedes' screw

Concrete mixer trucks are now as common as bulldozers and cranes. No building construction is complete without the help of these vehicles

DIGGERS, TRUCKS & EARTH MOVERS

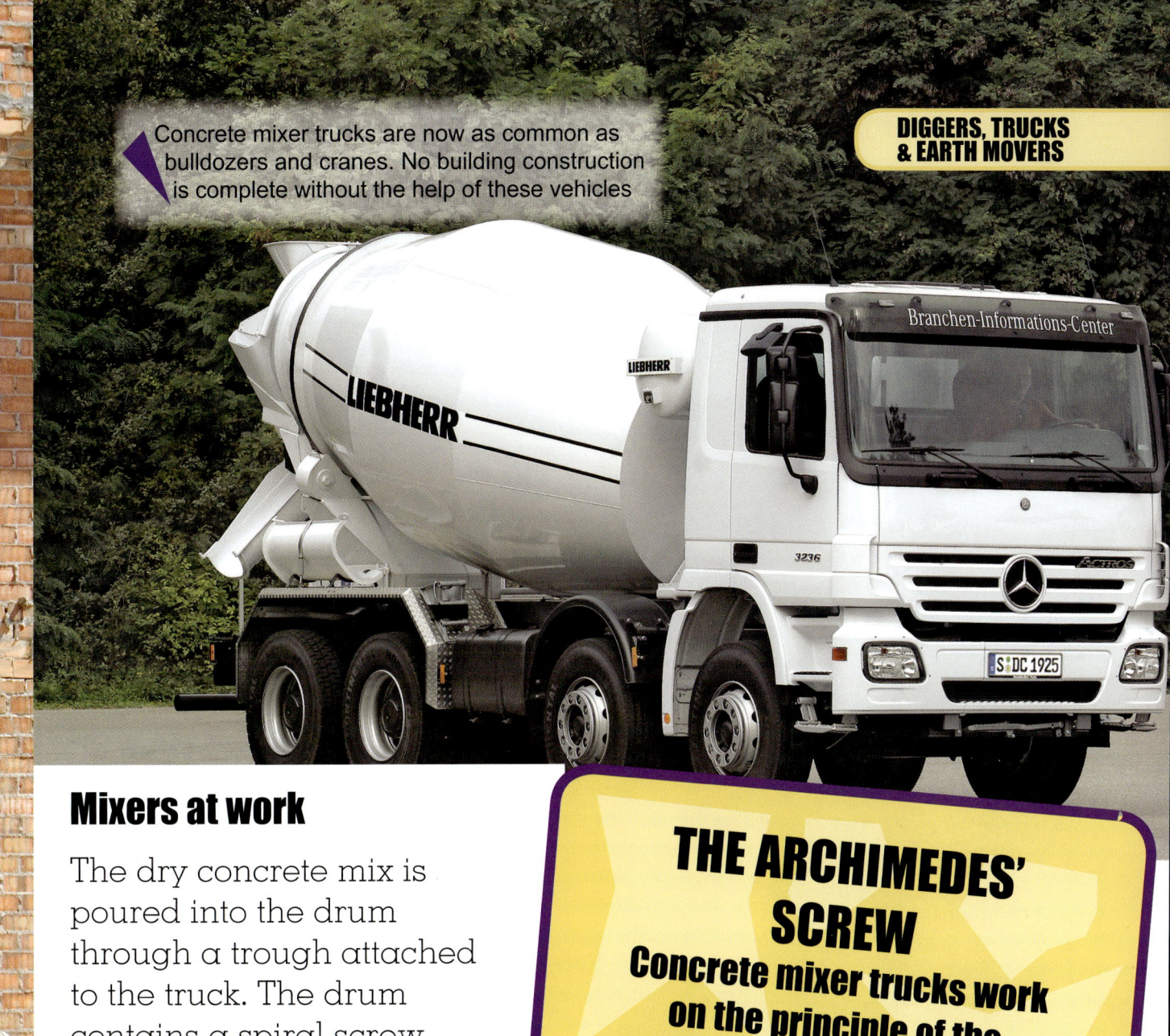

Mixers at work

The dry concrete mix is poured into the drum through a trough attached to the truck. The drum contains a spiral screw, which is used to mix the concrete and then to push it up and out of the drum by rotating the drum in the opposite direction.

THE ARCHIMEDES' SCREW

Concrete mixer trucks work on the principle of the Archimedes' screw, a simple machine devised by the Greek inventor Archimedes, to pump water up from low-lying areas. The machine comprises a screw placed inside a hollow pipe, one end of which is placed in water. The screw is then turned manually. The bottom end of the screw scoops up water which slides up the pipe and falls out of the top, as the screw turns.

SNOWPLOUGH

Some construction vehicles can be fitted with snowploughs to remove snow or ice from roads. However, in places that receive heavy snowfall, specialised snowploughing vehicles are used.

Removing snow

Small trucks or tractors, with a rectangular blade attached in front, are often used to clear snow from pavements and neighbourhood roads. Places with heavy snowfall use dump trucks with a wide, rectangular bucket in front that scoops up the snow and dumps it into the rear box. These trucks also carry salt and other chemicals to melt the snow.

▼ Snowplough trucks are often equipped with Global Positioning Systems and infrared cameras to help the driver find his way even during heavy snowfall

Snow blowers

A snow blower sucks in snow through the auger and blows it to one side through the impeller. They can be single stage or two-stage snow blowers. A single stage blower has only one auger to suck in the snow and discharge it. Two-stage blowers have two or more low-speed augers that suck in the snow and a high-speed impeller to discharge it.

▼ A two-stage snow blower

Auger

DIGGERS, TRUCKS & EARTH MOVERS

Rotary snowploughs

Rotary snowploughs remove snow from railway tracks. The plough consists of a large 'fan' that is propelled by diesel engines or electricity. One or more locomotives push the plough along the tracks while the blades of the fan cut through the snow and suck it in. The snow is then discharged to either side through output chutes at the top of the plough.

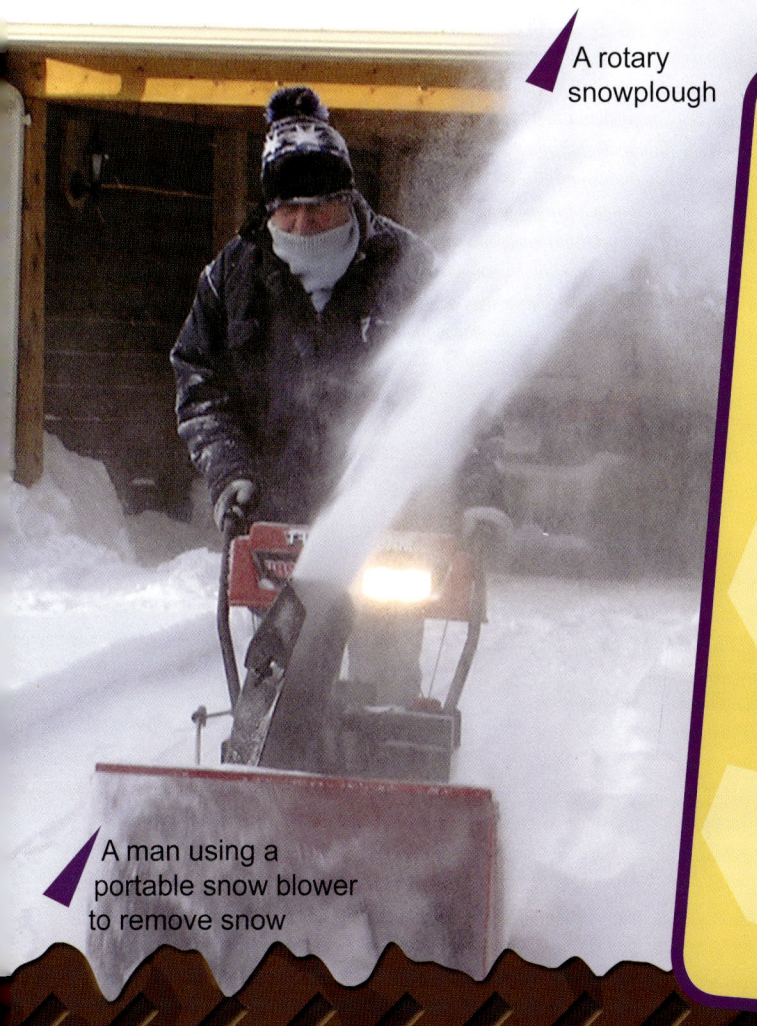

A rotary snowplough

A man using a portable snow blower to remove snow

FIGHTING ICE

Accidents on icy roads are one of the biggest dangers during winters. Some dump trucks are used specially for the purpose of making roads less slippery. These trucks carry salt, sand and other chemicals that are discharged through pumps to melt the ice. Loaders attached with rough rollers make roads less slippery by milling the icy surface.

ROAD CONSTRUCTION

Road construction requires specialised vehicles that help to flatten uneven surfaces and pave roads. Some of the most common construction vehicles, such as loaders and diggers, are used during road construction.

Graders

A grader consists of an engine and a cab at the rear, while a blade placed between the front and rear tyres is used to flatten uneven surfaces. They are largely used to prepare a base during road construction. Once the grader has done its work, the road is paved with other materials like asphalt.

▼ Graders are also used to maintain unpaved roads and create flat surfaces before building construction

Roller-compactors

Roller-compactors are popularly known as road-rollers. They are used to harden the ground for roads. After the grader has flattened the surface, the road-roller presses pebbles and stones into the ground. After pouring the asphalt, the road-roller is once again used to harden the road. The road-roller is really a tractor with a huge drum in the front. Smaller road-rollers are used for paving. They have a lever that can be operated by hand.

▼ Most road-rollers have one drum at the front. Some have two drums, one to the front and one to the rear

Making railway lines

Special vehicles are used in the construction and maintenance of railway tracks. A clearance car is used to make sure that trains travelling on a certain track do not face any obstruction. It consists of rods that extend in all directions and move to indicate any obstruction. A liner car is used to maintain the amount of stones and gravel between tracks. A tie-tamper presses gravel into the ground.

DIGGERS, TRUCKS & EARTH MOVERS

STEAMROLLERED!
The steamroller was the precursor to modern road-rollers. It comprised a large tractor with a heavy, iron cylinder that worked as front wheel, much like the modern road-roller. Steamrollers were powered by steam engines.

▶ A tie-tamper being used to press the ties, or sleepers, into the gravel between the tracks

▶ Steamrollers like this one were once used to pave roads. These road-rollers were powered by steam and were slow compared to modern rollers

FORESTRY VEHICLES

Sometimes, large parts of a forest or woods have to be cleared to make way for new buildings, roads, railway lines or bridges. This is done using special vehicles like feller bunchers, harvesters, skidders and forwarders.

▼ A harvester can either be wheeled or tracked, depending on the kind of surface it is used on

Harvesters

Harvesters cut trees and trim their branches. They are widely used throughout the world to fell trees. A harvester head consists of a hydraulic chainsaw that cuts the tree. It is attached to the boom on the vehicle. It also has curved, de-limbing knives used to remove branches from the trunk. A pair of feed-rollers helps to grasp the tree while

Feller bunchers

Some countries use a vehicle called a feller buncher instead of a harvester. This vehicle has a circular saw that spins to cut through the tree. Some feller bunchers have a shear-like device that can be used to cut small trees. A mechanical hand holds the tree at its base while cutting.

▼ Unlike harvesters, feller bunchers do not remove the branches

DIGGERS, TRUCKS & EARTH MOVERS

SKIDDERS OF THE PAST

During the nineteenth century, skidders consisted of a cart pulled by horses or mules. The cart was positioned over the logs that had to be transported. A pair of tongs was used to lift one end of the log. The cart was then pulled forward, causing the log to "skid" along the ground, giving the vehicle its name.

Moving logs

Once the trees are cut, they are transported from the site using forwarders. A forwarder consists of a crane that picks up the logs and places them on a carrier attached to the driver's cab. In places where feller bunchers cut trees, skidders are used for the job. A skidder is a wheeled tractor with a winch to drag logs. It has a small blade in the front to push logs out of the way.

◀ Forwarders are usually used along with harvesters

◀ Some skidders have a hydraulic grapple that lifts one end of the logs to drag them to the collection point, where they are loaded on to trucks

93

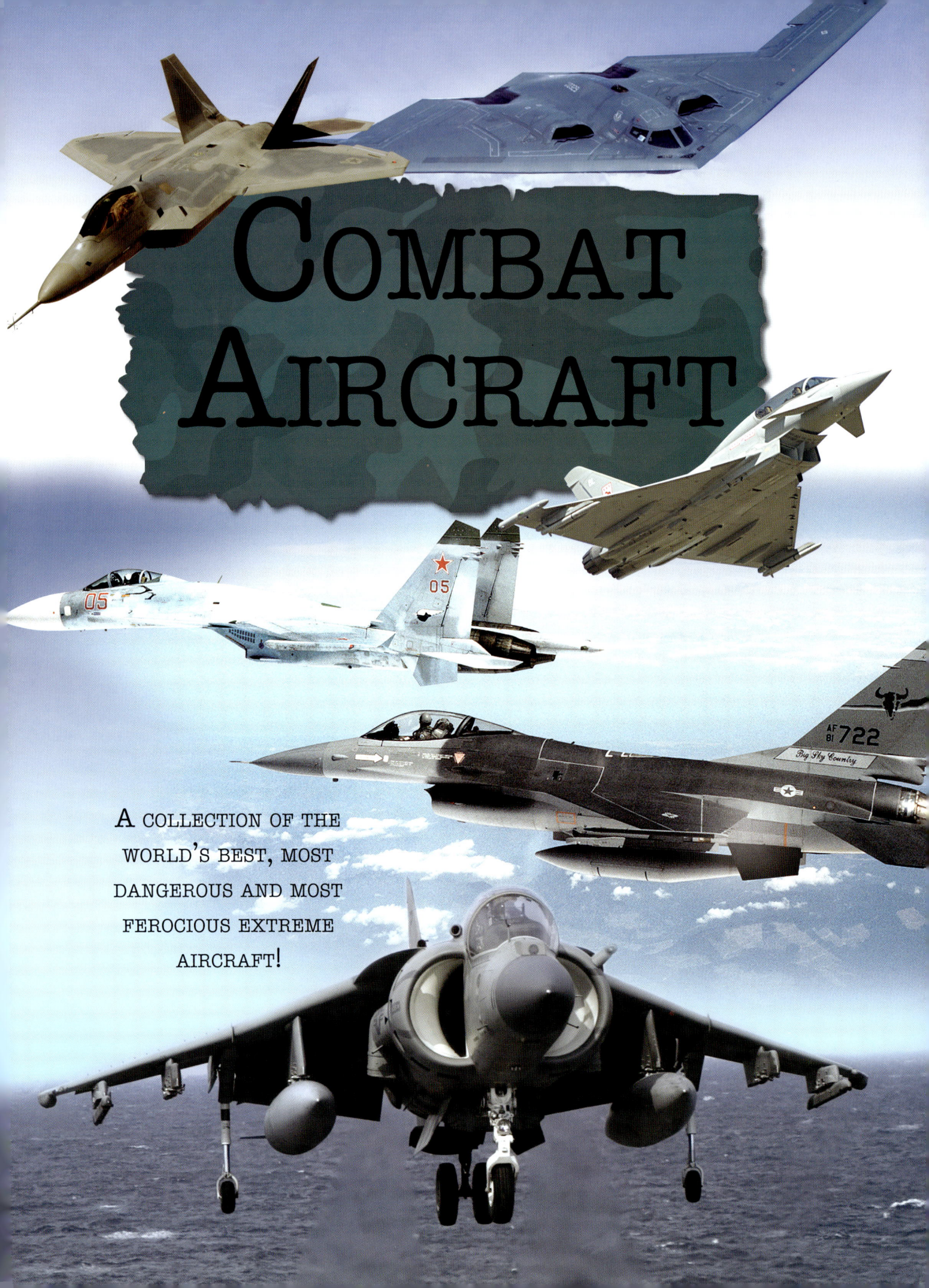

Combat Aircraft

A collection of the world's best, most dangerous and most ferocious extreme aircraft!

Know Your Combat Aircraft

Combat aircraft are aeroplanes used by the military during war. Aeroplanes came to be used for military purposes within a few years of the first flight of a heavier-than-air aircraft in 1903. Hot air balloons and zeppelins were used before this to gather information about enemy troops.

Types of combat aircraft

Combat aircraft can be broadly divided into fighter, bomber, tanker, trainer, surveillance and transport aircraft. Fighters and bombers carry weapons and are directly involved in combat missions. Fighter planes are designed mainly to fight other aircraft. They are small, fast and easy to manoeuvre. Bombers are used to drop bombs on targets on the ground, such as buildings and bridges.

Unarmed combat aircraft

Apart from fighters and bombers, air forces of the world also employ other types of aircraft that do not carry weapons. Some, like tankers, carry fuel to other attack aircraft, while others, such as transport aircraft, carry troops and equipment from one place to another. Surveillance or reconnaissance aircraft fly over the enemy targets and take pictures of their troops and facilities. Lastly, there are trainer aircrafts, which are used to train pilots.

Combat helicopters

Helicopters are also an important part of any defence force. Like fixed wing aircraft, combat helicopters are also of various kinds. Attack helicopters carry machine guns and missiles to fight enemy troops. Some attack helicopters are equipped with air-to-air missiles for defensive purposes. Attack helicopters are mainly used to provide air support for ground troops. Transport helicopters are used to move men and machinery. Helicopters can also be used to drop supplies and paratroopers, and carry out search and rescue missions. Since helicopters can take-off and land from just about anywhere, they are often preferred to fixed wing aircraft in war zones.

World War I Fighters

Fighter aircraft were first developed during World War I, starting with the aerial bombing of Turkish troops by the Italians in 1911. However, despite rapid technological advance in aviation, most of the early World War I aircraft were used for reconnaissance purposes. The first true fighter plane emerged almost a year after the war began.

A daring mission

The biggest challenge faced by the designers of early fighters was the positioning of the aircraft's guns. The ideal position for the gun was between the pilot and the nose of the aircraft, as this enabled easy firing as well as repairing, if the gun jammed. However, this was impossible as the fired bullets would strike the propeller. Roland Garros, a French pilot, overcame this problem by attaching protective metal wedges to the wooden propeller blades. Garros shot down three German planes using this improved fighter.

Fokker's design

On April 18, 1915, Garros and his fighter was shot down and captured by the Germans. The famous German aircraft designer Anthony Fokker studied the captured plane in detail. He then introduced the interrupter gear, which would allow the gun to fire between the blades of the spinning propeller. This device was fitted to the Fokker E-1 monoplanes that terrorised the Allied forces. The innovation was so successful that the period was known as the Fokker Scourge.

Fokker D.VII
Manufactured by: Fokker Aeroplanbau, Germany
Crew: Single
Maximum speed: 186 km/h (116 mph)
Weapons: Two machine guns

Roland Garros improvised his Morane-Saulnier Type L fighter by attaching metal wedges to its propellers

Fighters of Allied forces

In 1916 France introduced the Nieuport 17 and Britain its first fighter, the Sopwith 1 1/2 Strutter. They were inspired by a Fokker plane that was forced to land in enemy territory due to fog. The British and the French conducted detailed studies of the captured plane and developed better combat aircraft. The Nieuport 17, a biplane fighter, had a powerful engine and large wings. In fact, it was so good that it was soon adopted by all the Allied air forces.

Morane-Saulnier Type L

Manufactured by: Morane-Saulnier, France
Crew: One or two
Maximum speed: 115 km/h (71 mph)
Weapons: One machine gun

The Sopwith 1 1/2 Strutter was the first British aircraft to be built with interrupter gear

Sopwith 1 1/2 Strutter

Manufactured by: Sopwith Aviation Company, U.K.
Crew: Two
Maximum speed: 164 km/h (102 mph)
Weapons: Two machine guns; up to 100 kg (224 lb) of bomb

When the Allied forces developed aircraft similar to the E-1 the Germans came up with a more advanced fighter – the Fokker D.VII. This plane was introduced in 1918 leading to a second Fokker Scourge

European Bombers of WWII

During World War II, the countries involved realised that to defeat the enemy it was vital to strike at its industries, military bases and dams. Since such targets were often deep in enemy territory, only long-range bombers could carry out these tasks, making them the ultimate weapons of war.

British bombers

Britain had some of the best bombers at its service, including the Avro Lancaster and de Havilland Mosquito. The most notable mission of the Lancaster was the bombing of the Ruhr Valley dams in North Rhine-Westphalia, Germany. The Mosquito was a light and speedy aircraft, useful as a day or night fighter. Other bombers included the sturdy but slow Wellington, with which Britain began the World War.

Avro Lancaster
Manufactured by: Avro, U.K.
Crew: Seven
Maximum speed: 448 km/h (280 mph)
Weapons: Eight machine guns; up to 10,000 kg (22,000 lb) bombs

The Avro Lancaster was the main night bomber of the Royal Air Force. This bomber had a huge bay to carry bombs and the most advanced communication systems of the time

German bombers

The Junkers were the mainstay of the German bomber line-up. The Ju 88 was a medium range bomber that could carry a great deal of ammunition. It was also an excellent night fighter. The Heinkel 111, a medium range bomber, was also widely used until the end of the war. The Heinkel was especially effective during the first phase of the London Blitz. The Junkers 87 Stuka dive bombers, yet another favourite, was used extensively during the Battle of Britain.

OTHER BOMBERS

The Petlyakov 2 was the best Russian bomber in the war. It was fast and agile. Russia's long-range bomber, the Ilyushin 4, was used to devastate Berlin, East Germany, and German-occupied territory in Eastern Europe and Russia. Another major bomber of the time was the Italian Savoya-Marchetti 79. This light bomber could carry a considerable amount of ammunition and was used mainly as a torpedo bomber.

> The Stuka dive bombers had wind-powered sirens fixed to their wheels. These sirens wailed as wind struck them during dives, designed to scare the enemy. The wailing sirens earned the bombers the nickname, "Trumpets of Jericho"

Junkers Ju 87

Manufactured by: Junkers Flugzeug und Motorenwerke AG, GErmany
Crew: Two
Speed: 310 km/hour (193 mph)
Weapons: Three machine guns; one 250kg (551lb) bomb

The Attack on Pearl Harbor

At first, the United States decided to keep out of World War II. However, the Japanese were worried about the presence of the U.S. Navy in the Pacific. On December 7, 1941, the Japanese launched an air attack on the American fleet at Pearl Harbor to eliminate this danger.

Mighty carriers

Huge ships carrying combat aircraft had been introduced into the navies of all major countries following World War I. Aircraft carriers were, however, tested for the first time during the Pearl Harbor attack. Over 350 Japanese planes, in two groups, attacked the U.S. naval base. The first group mainly targeted the U.S. naval ships, while the second group bombed airfields on the island. By the end of the attack, the U.S. lost more than 2,400 men, almost all their combat aircraft and eight battleships.

Japanese bombers bombarding U.S. naval vessels and airstrip at the Pearl Harbor

Japanese Zeroes

The Japanese did not have a separate air force during the war. Instead, combat aircraft were an extended part of both the Japanese army and navy. The naval air service was stronger and well known for its Mitsubishi Zeroes, which played an important role in the Pearl Harbor attack. The Model 21 Zeroes were specially built for use on board aircraft carriers.

The bombers

The Zeroes were supported by the Aichi D3A dive-bombers, codenamed 'Val'. Later on, it was replaced by the more powerful Yokosuka D4Y Suisei. Special Japanese fighter units called Kamikaze, or Divine Wind, conducted suicide attacks on enemy ships. The Yokosuka D4Y Suisei and Nakajima Ki-115 were widely used for such attacks. During the war, about 2,800 Kamikaze attacks sunk 34 U.S. ships and damaged 368 others.

A6M2 Zero
Manufactured by: Mitsubishi, Japan
Type: single-seat fighter-bomber
Maximum speed: 540 km/h (336 mph)
Weapons: Two machine guns; two cannons: up to 60 kg (132 lb) bombs; two 250 kg (551 lb) kamikaze bombs

The Mitsubishi Zeroes were highly manoeuvrable and had great firepower

The Aichi D3A carrier-borne dive bomber played a major role in the Pearl Harbor attack. They were also used in kamikaze missions towards the end of the war

Aichi D3A
Manufactured by: Aichi Kokuki KK, Japan
Type: Two-seat dive bomber
Maximum speed: 386 km/h (240 mph)
Weapons: Three machine guns; two 60 kg (132 lb) bombs; one fixed 250 kg (551 lb) bomb

ENTER THE AMERICANS

The devastation at Pearl Harbor greatly angered the Americans. The decision to stay out of the war was reversed. The U.S. declared war on Japan, and shortly afterwards on Germany. The course of World War II was greatly influenced by the superior planes developed by the U.S.

EARLY AMERICAN FIGHTERS

The U.S. had a good collection of fighter aircraft even at the time of the Pearl Harbor attack. However, the Japanese strategy of surprise attacks on the U.S. air bases prevented them from responding quickly. The only resistance came from P-36 Hawks and P-40 Warhawks. The P-40 was used extensively by Allied forces across the world. It was sturdy and more efficient than most of its Japanese counterparts, but could not fly very high.

Curtiss P-40E
Manufactured by: Curtiss-Wright Corporation, U.S.A.
Type: Single seat fighter-bomber
Maximum speed: 583 km/h (362 mph)
Weapons: Six machine guns; 317 kg (700 lb) bombs

Over 13,700 P-40 fighters were produced during the war. They were used by 28 countries

THE STAR FIGHTERS

Other major fighters used during the war were the Grumman F6F Hellcat and the Lockheed P-38 Lightning, both were more than a match for the light Japanese planes. The carrier-based Hellcat was in fact responsible for 75 per cent of all aerial victories by the U.S. in the Pacific Ocean. The other U.S. fighter to leave its mark on the war was the P-51 Mustang. The P-51 played a vital role in defeating the Luftwaffe and giving the Allied forces complete air superiority over Germany.

P-51 Mustang
Manufactured by: North American Aviation, U.S.A.
Type: Single-seat, bomber escort, fighter-bomber
Maximum speed: 704 km/h (437 mph)
Weapons: Six machine guns; up to 907 kg (2,000 lb) bombs; ten rockets

B-29 Superfortress (Enola Gay)

Manufactured by: Boeing IDS, U.S.A.
Type: Ten crew, four-engine heavy bomber
Maximum speed: 587 km/hour (365 mph)
Weapons: 12 machine guns; one cannon; 9,072 kg (20,000 lb) bombs

The B-29 Superfortress, named *Enola Gay*, became the first aircraft in history to drop an atomic bomb. The aircraft dropped the atomic bomb, *Little Boy* over Hiroshima on August 6, 1945

Bombers to the fore

The American strategy in World War II was to rely heavily on its bombers. Intially, the unescorted bombers suffered huge losses due to enemy firing. Later, when the P-51 Mustang, the first long-range fighter, accompanied bombing squads fewer U.S. bombers were shot down. In the Pacific the U.S. Air Force used the B-29 Superfortress to launch attacks on Japan from China. The B-29 was also used to drop the first atomic bombs over the Japanese cities of Hiroshima and Nagasaki, in August 1945.

The P-51 Mustang was one of the most successful combat aircraft of World War II

Flying into the Jet Age

The first jet-powered combat aircraft was the German Messerschmitt Me 262 built during World War II. After the war, the British took the lead. Within a few years Britain had several jet fighters, two naval jets and even a jet-powered seaplane.

Initial lead

Britain was the only Allied power to have a jet fighter squadron before the end of the war. The Gloster Meteors of the Royal Air Force defended Britain from German V-1 bombs. Britain also introduced the single-engine de Havilland DH-100 Vampire in 1946. The Sea Vampire was the first jet aircraft to operate from an aircraft carrier. Apart from developing several other jet aircraft, the British also built a single seat jet seaplane called the "Squirt" which however, never took to air.

Gloster Meteor
Manufactured by: Gloster Aircraft Company, U.K.
Crew: One
Maximum speed: 668 km/hour (415 mph)
Weapons: Four cannons

The Gloster Meteor was only the second jet-powered fighter in history. It was extensively used during the Korean War in 1950

P-80 Shooting Stars were slowly replaced by the more effective F-86 Sabres as, the former were not advanced enough to face the much superior Russian aircraft

American efforts

The United States entered the jet age in 1942 with their Bell XP-59. However, this fighter was never used in combat. The first American jet fighter to see action was the Lockheed P-80 Shooting Star. This jet-powered combat aircraft was used extensively in the Korean War. The Republic F-84 was another first generation jet-powered fighter that served with distinction in the Korean War. However, the most successful combat aircraft of the jet age to serve in the Korean War was undoubtedly the F-86A Sabre.

P-80 Shooting Star
Manufactured by: Lockheed Martin, USA
Crew: One
Maximum speed: 966 km/h (601 mph)
Weapons: Six machine guns; two 454 kg (1001 lb) bombs; 10-16 rockets

Russian response

Russia was quick to realise that it would need to enter the jet age to keep up with military technology. Four design teams took up the challenge to produce the first Russian jet combat aircraft. Two of them came up with prototypes within six months. On April 24, 1946, Artem Mikoyan and Mikhail Gurevich won the contest and their MiG-9 became the first Russian jet to fly. It was followed by the Yakovlev Yak-15.

Messerschmitt Me 262

Manufactured by: Messerschmitt-Blkow-Blohm, Germany
Crew: One
Maximum speed: 870 km/h (540 mph)
Weapons: Four cannons; 454 kg (1000lb) bombs; 24 rockets

The jet-powered Messerschmitt Me 262 was not very successful during the war, but it was responsible for the subsequent revolution in aircraft design

The MiG-9 was mainly used in ground attacks as the aircraft design had many problems and its performance was poor

Supersonic Fighters

After the jet age, the next milestone was to get combat aircraft to fly faster than the speed of sound. Guided missiles were also first developed at this time. The early supersonic aircraft gave up agility and bomb carrying capacity in favour of speed and the ability to gain height rapidly.

The F-100 Super Sabre deployed in Vietnam was later replaced by F-4 and F-105 fighter-bombers

F-100 Super Sabre

Manufactured by:	North American Aviation, U.S.A.
Crew:	One
Maximum speed:	1,390 km/h (864 mph)
Weapons:	Four cannons; up to 3,190 kg (7,033 lb) of bombs; missiles and rockets

Breaking the sound barrier

The F-100 Super Sabre was the first U.S. fighter capable of supersonic speed. It broke the sound barrier on its first flight and set a speed record in October 1953 at 1,215 km/h (755.149 mph). The Super Sabre, especially its F-100D variant, was widely used in the Vietnam War. The MiG-19 was the first Soviet combat aircraft to break the sound barrier. Production of MiG-19s first started in 1954, and some continue in service to this day. The English Electric Lightning of Britain is remembered for the fact that it held the world air-speed record for being over twice the speed of sound.

Improved designs

Achieving speeds faster than sound was just the first step towards a new generation of fighters. Aircraft designers had to improve performance and efficiency to cope with the challenges of the modern world. Swing-wings were developed to reduce friction and increase speed. This innovation helped the aircraft to sweep its wings back during high speeds and at the same time bring it back to the normal position in lower speeds.

New Age Controls

Increased speeds naturally led to the development of super light aircraft. Weapons were made lighter and lightweight metal alloys were used to build these fighters. Another significant change came with fly-by wire control systems. These systems use computers to control the aircraft, thereby getting rid of heavy cables. Modern fighters also have light and responsive controls, which make them more agile and easy to manoeuvre.

The Su-27 was one of the first aircraft to be built with high amounts of titanium making the huge aircraft much lighter. It was also the first Soviet combat aircraft to have fly-by-wire controls

Sukhoi Su-27

Manufactured by: Sukhoi Design Bureau, Russia
Crew: One
Maximum speed: 2,494 km/h (1,550 mph)
Weapons: 1 cannon; up to 6,000 kg (13,228 lb) of missiles and bombs

The F-14 Tomcat was one of the first fighters to have swing wings. The aircraft was agile and proved very effective as an interceptor

F-14 Tomcat

Manufactured by: Grumman Aerospace Corporation, U.S.A.
Crew: Two
Maximum speed: 2,485 km/h (1,544 mph)
Weapons: One cannon; air-to-air missiles; iron bombs

107

Supersonic Bombers

After supersonic fighters it was the turn of the bombers to break the sound barrier. The Convair B-58 Hustler was the world's first supersonic bomber, capable of flying over targets at Mach 2 (twice the speed of sound).

B-58 Hustler

The B-58 Hustler, of the U.S. Airforce, was a revolutionary bomber in more ways than one. One of its unique features was a tailless delta wing that helped the aircraft to reduce friction. The wing also enabled the aircraft to achieve high speeds even at low altitudes. The most amazing feature of the B-58 was its ejection capsule, which made it possible for the crew to eject out of the bomber even while travelling at twice the speed of sound. The normal ejection seats of that time did not have this ability.

B-58 Hustler
Manufactured by: Consolidated Vultee Aircraft Corporation (Convair), U.S.A.
Crew: Five
Maximum speed: 2,126 km/h (1,321 mph)
Weapons: One cannon; up to 640kg (1,400 lb) of conventional and nuclear bombs

Despite its exceptional performance, the B-58 Hustler was retired by 1970 due to its high cost and maintenance

Other American bombers

The B-1 Lancer is the backbone of the long-range bomber force belonging to the U.S. Air Force. It has been used in several successful operations led by the U.S., including the ones in Iraq, Kosovo and Afghanistan. This bomber also has variable geometry wings, which means that the angle of its wings can be changed at different times while the aircraft is in flight.

B-1 Lancer
Manufactured by: Boeing IDS, U.S.A.
Crew: Four
Maximum speed: 1,329 km/h (825.31 mph)
Weapons: up to 34,000 kg (74,957 lb) of bombs

The B-1 Lancer has been highly successful during Operation Enduring Freedom in Afghanistan and Operation Iraqi Freedom

Soviet bombers

The Tupolev Tu-22M also has wings, which can be swept back when it is flying faster than the speed of sound. The Soviets used the Tu-22M extensively in their war in Afghanistan for carpet bombing (dropping a shower of bombs). The Tu-22M is designed to carry conventional as well nuclear bombs. However, the Tupolev Tu-160 is perhaps the most successful supersonic bomber developed by the Soviet Union. This bomber resembles the American B-1 Lancer but is much larger and faster than the American bomber. It is also the heaviest combat aircraft ever built. The Tu-160 has swing-wings and fly-by-wire controls. This bomber replaced the Tu-22M and continues to be used by Russia and other former Soviet nations.

Tu-22M

Manufactured by: Tupolev Design Bureau, Russia
Crew: Four
Maximum speed: 2,160 km/hour (1,350 mph)
Weapons: One cannon; up to 24,000 kg (52,910 lb) of bombs

During the Cold War, the threat posed by the Tu-22M bomber was such that the U.S government increased the country's defence budget to help build equally advanced bombers and fighters

Modern Combat Aircraft

The demands of modern warfare require strong, efficient, agile and up-to-date combat aircraft – all at low cost and low maintenance. The latest developments include glass cockpits, thrust vectoring, supercruise, stealth technology and use of lightweight materials like alloys, glass and plastic.

Sukhoi Su-30 MKI
Manufactured by: Corporation (Russia) and Hindustan Aeronautics Ltd (India)
Crew: Two
Maximum speed: 1,350 km/hour (839 mph)
Weapons: One 30 mm cannon; 14 missiles

The Sukhoi Su-30 MKI is a highly manoeuvrable fighter with thrust vectoring

Supercruise

Supercruising aircraft can fly faster than the speed of sound without afterburners. Afterburners use up a lot of fuel and reduce flying time. The first aircraft to go supersonic in level flight, without afterburners, was the English Electric Lightning. All modern combat aircraft, like the Eurofighter Typhoon and the F-22 Raptor are supercruisers. Thrust vectoring technology endows modern fighters with eye-popping agility, allowing them to make 90-degree turns.

The Nighthawk is made of radar absorbing materials and paints, and also has a unique shape that makes it almost undetectable to radar.

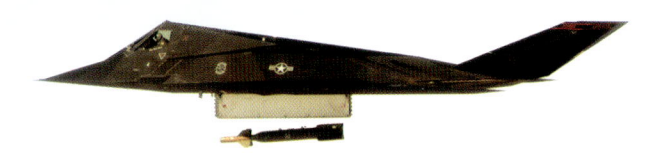

Stealth

Lockheed's F-117 Nighthawk was the first combat aircraft to use stealth technology successfully in overcoming detection by radar. However, it can carry very little fuel and weapons, and also does not have a radar of its own. Efforts are on to counter these problems, especially since stealth combat aircraft are expected to play an important role in future conflicts.

F-117 Nighthawk
Manufactured by: Lockheed Aeronautical Systems Co, U.S.A.
Crew: One
Maximum speed: 1,127 km/h (700 mph)
Weapons: up to 2,268 kg (5,000 lb) of bombs or missiles

Glass cockpits

Early aircraft cockpits were often crammed with dozens of dials and gauges that needed to be constantly monitored. Glass cockpits have just a few computer controlled displays of all the information that the pilot needs. In the F-15A Eagle, all important information is projected on the screen in front of the pilot. This enables the pilot to track down and shoot enemy aircraft without taking his eyes off it.

The F-15 Eagle was one of the first aircraft to have a Head-Up display system that projected flight information on a screen in front of the pilot

F-15A Eagle

Manufactured by: Boeing (formerly McDonnell-Douglas), U.S.A.
Crew: One
Speed: 2,575 km/h (1,600 mph)
Weapons: One cannon; eight missiles; up to 7,300 kg (16094 lb) of bombs

NAVAL COMBAT AIRCRAFT

Naval aviation began in 1912, when, for the first time, an aircraft took off from the British warship, HMS *Hibernia*. Today, naval aviation stands shoulder to shoulder with its air force counterpart.

CARRIER-BASED AIRCRAFT

Aircraft carriers are very large, but even so it is not easy to take off or land a plane on a ship, especially if it is moving. Carrier-based combat aircraft are usually small, with foldable wings, as there is a lack of space on carriers. They take off in the direction the ship is sailing and land from the rear. Some carriers have a steam-powered catapult that pushes the aircraft forward with force, allowing it to take off quickly. All aircraft that take off and land by taxiing have a tail hook attached to their tail. The tail hook is a claw-like device that grabs the thick arrestor wires stretched across the ship's deck as the aircraft lands, forcing the aircraft to halt.

The picture shows a combat aircraft getting ready for take off from the deck of a carrier

MODERN CARRIER AIRCRAFT

VTOL, or Vertical Take off and Landing reduces the risk of taking off or landing on ships. With VTOL, combat aircraft can lift up without taxiing, much like a helicopter. Aircraft are able to do this using the thrust vector technology, which enables the aircraft to direct the thrust from the main engines in any direction.

The Yakovlev Yak-38 was the Soviet Union's only VTOL combat aircraft. This aircraft could be guided by computer systems to land on the deck of the carrier without any help from the pilot

Yak-38
Manufactured by: Yakovlev Design Bureau, Russia
Crew: One
Maximum speed: 1050 km/hour (652mph)
Weapons: One cannon, 1,000 kg (2,200 lb) of bombs

Ski-jump ramps

The biggest drawback of Vertical Take Off and Landing aircraft is that they cannot carry a great deal of weight. This is very important, as combat aircraft need to carry enough fuel and weapons for long-range operations. Ski jump runways provide the perfect solution for this problem. In this case, combat aircraft can take off normally, without catapults, as these short runways provide the necessary power. Moreover, in such instances, the aircraft can land vertically and avoid the use of arrestor wires.

AV-8B Harrier II
Manufactured by: McDonnell Douglas, U.S.A.
Crew: One
Maximum speed: 1000 km/h (629 mph)
Weapons: One cannon; up to 5,987 kg (13,200 lb) of bombs and missiles

The AV-8B Harrier II is a V/STOL, or Vertical/Short Take-off and Landing, aircraft. It usually takes off from a carrier vertically, but is also capable of taking off with the help of a ski jump when the load is too heavy for a vertical take-off

Helicopters in Combat

Helicopters were first used for military purposes soon after they were invented in the early 1900s. The U.S. Army Air Corps asked Igor Sikorsky, a helicopter manufacturer, to develop a model for them.

XR-4

Type:	Two-seat, training and rescue
Manufactured by:	Sikorsky Aircraft Corporation, USA
Speed:	131 km/h (81 mph)
Maximum weight at take-off:	1,150 kg (2,535 lb)

The Black Hawk has featured in many blockbuster films including *Clear and Present Danger* and *Black Hawk Down*

In 1942, Sikorsky developed the XR-4 for the U.S. military. It was the world's first mass produced helicopter and also the first to use a single rotor

Attack helicopters

Attack helicopters are used in much the same way as attack aircraft are. These helicopters support troops on the ground by targeting enemy troops and tanks. Some helicopters like the Black Hawk often carry air-to-air missiles to attack enemy helicopters or aircraft. Naval attack helicopters, like the Sea Hawk, can be used to target enemy ships and even detect and destroy submarines.

Troop carriers

Helicopters are often used to transport troops to and from battlefields. Some like the CH-47 Chinook or the Mi-6 'Hook' can carry dozens of fully equipped troops. They can also be used to quickly airlift injured troops to the nearest hospital.

Mil Mi-6 Hook

Type:	Five-seat heavy transport helicopter
Manufactured by:	Mil Moscow Helicopter Plant, Russia
Crew:	Five
Maximum speed:	300 km/hour (186 mph)
Maximum weight at take off:	41,700 kg (91,933 lb)

The Mi-6 was used for both military and civilian purposes. It could carry about 60 troops, or up to 12,000 kg of load. The Mi-6 continues to be used in some countries including China, Russia and Egypt

Sky crane helicopters

From their earliest days, helicopters have been used to lift men, weapons and machinery into the heart of the war zone. Helicopters like the CH-54 'Skycrane' or the Mi-10 'Harke'-B have little by way of a body, apart from the cockpit, the engine and the rotors, but their engines are powerful enough to lift several tonnes at a time. The CH-54 was often used in the Vietnam War to lift as many as 100 troops.

The CH-54 could also lift portable hospitals or tanks. Such helicopters were also used to retrieve aircraft that had been shot down

CH-54

Type: Three-seat heavy-lift crane
Manufactured by: Sikorsky Aircraft Corporation, U.S.A.
Maximum speed: 370 km/h (230 mph)
Maximum weight at take off: 21,319 kg (47,000 lb)

American Combat Helicopters

The United States has pioneered the development of helicopters for both civilian and military uses. Most of the major helicopter manufacturers, like Sikorsky, Bell and Boeing, are American. Helicopters have been a major part of the U.S. Army, Air Force, Navy and Marines ever since World War II.

Heavy duty helicopters

Large helicopters in the United States military, like the CH-53E Super Stallion, can lift nearly 17 tonnes of cargo. This enables them to lift armoured vehicles along with their crew! They are also helpful in retrieving downed aircraft. In fact, the Super Stallion, which is used by the U.S. Navy and Marines, can retrieve almost any aircraft.

The two rotors of the CH-47 Chinook give the helicopter extra power to lift loads as heavy as a tank

CH-47 Chinook
Manufactured by: Boeing IDS, U.S.A.
Crew: Three
Maximum speed: 296 km/h (184 mph)
Weapons: None
Capacity: 30 troops

Helicopters in combat

The attack helicopters of the United States come armed with a variety of weapons. A top-of-the-line ground attack helicopter like Boeing's AH-64 Apache can fight a battalion of tanks with its 16 anti-tank missiles and 76 rockets. It can target ground troops with rapid-fire bursts from its 30 mm chain gun. However, despite its power, a helicopter can never match the speed of a fighter or the range of a bomber.

The AH-64 Apache is the main combat helicopter of the U.S. Army. It has seen combat in many conflicts including the Gulf War, Operation Enduring Freedom in Afghanistan and Operation Iraqi Freedom

Various models of the Sea Hawk have been developed for specific roles from troop transport and search and rescue missions, to anti-submarine warfare and ground attacks

SH-60 Sea Hawk

Manufactured by:	Sikorsky Aircraft Corporation, U.S.A.
Crew:	Three
Maximum speed:	233 km/h (145 mph)
Weapons:	One machine gun; two torpedoes

AH-64 Apache

Manufactured by:	Boeing IDS, U.S.A.
Type:	Two-seat attack helicopter
Maximum speed:	449 km/hour (279 mph)
Weapons:	One cannon; missiles and rockets

HELICOPTERS IN THE U.S. NAVY

The ease with which helicopters can take off and land from warships of all kinds gives them an edge over fixed wing combat aircraft. Apart from the usual roles of transporting troops, naval helicopters also have other uses. Some helicopters like the Sea Hawk or the Sea Knight are also used in search and rescue operations and in anti-submarine warfare. These helicopters have very sophisticated radar systems that enable them to detect objects under water, which they can then target and destroy using depth charges and torpedoes. Some are used to drop supplies, transport weapons and carry out medical evacuation.

European Combat Helicopters

The helicopter manufacturing industry in Europe has grown rapidly. In fact, today, the largest and the fastest combat helicopters are made outside the U.S. The Aerospatiale in France and the British Westland are some of the world's leading combat helicopter manufacturers.

Russian helicopters

The Mil Helicopter Design Bureau's Mi-26 'Halo' is the largest combat helicopter in the world. It weighs 28 tonnes when empty and can lift 28 tonnes of cargo. It has two turboshaft engines that give the aircraft a powerful lift. The Mil Moscow Helicopter Plant also makes one of the fastest combat helicopters, the Mi-24 'Hind'. This gunship has a heavily armoured body to withstand enemy fire.

Mil Mi-24 Hind
- Manufactured by: Mil Moscow Helicopter Plant, Russia
- Crew: Two
- Maximum speed: 335 km/h (208 mph)
- Weapons: One cannon; up to 2,400 kg (5,291 lb) of bombs, missiles and rockets

Even the rotor blades of the Mi-24 are made of titanium to endure cannon fire

British helicopters

The Westland Lynx is Britain's top attack helicopter. It is used in both the Army Air Corps and the Royal Navy's Fleet Air Arm. Westland's Sea King and its Commando variant have the longest range amongst all combat helicopters outside the United States. The Sea King is used by the Royal Navy for anti-submarine warfare and as an airborne early warning system.

French helicopters

The French anti-tank attack helicopter SA 341 Gazelle is one of the fastest combat helicopters in the world. Its speed results from its light weight. The Gazelle is also used for a variety of other operations including directing ground attack aircraft, medical evacuation, directing artillery fire and communications. Another popularly used French helicopter is the Aérospatiale Super Frelon. This helicopter has the longest range in the French military. It can fly up to 1,000 kilometres. The Super Frelon's sturdy build and long range makes it useful as a heavy-duty transport helicopter. Anti-submarine and anti-ship variants of the Super Frelon were also produced.

The Lynx was initially developed as a utility helicopter for both civilian and naval purposes. It was later modified as an attack helicopter for the army and the navy

Sea King

Manufactured by: Westland Helicopters, U.K.
Crew: Two to Four
Maximum speed: 232 km/h (144 mph)
Weapons: Four depth charges or torpedoes

SA 341 Gazelle

Manufactured by: Aerospatiale (France) and Westland Aircraft (U.K.) joint venture
Crew: One or two
Maximum speed: 311 km/hour (193 mph)
Weapons: Up to two machine guns or one cannon; missiles or rockets

The Gazelle is one of the fastest helicopters ever. It has seen service in all branches of the British armed forces as an attack helicopter, trainer and transport helicopter

COMBAT AIRCRAFT OF THE FUTURE

The future belongs to multi-role combat aircraft, with all the features of present fighters and more. Some new generation aircraft with extraordinary agility and dogfight abilities include the F-22 Raptor, Joint Strike Fighter, Rafale and Eurofighter Typhoon.

FACE OF THE FUTURE

The F-22 Raptor, of the U.S. Air Force, is the face of future combat aircraft. This fighter has it all – stealth technology, computerised control systems, high manoeuvrability, supercruise and thrust vectoring. However, its most outstanding feature is its unique radar that can track several targets even in the worst weather conditions, while confusing enemy sensors at the same time. This makes the F-22 Raptor a powerful fighter.

F-22 Raptor
Manufactured by: Lockheed Martin Aeronautics and Boeing IDS, U.S.A.
Crew: Single
Maximum speed: 2,450 km/h (1,522 mph)
Weapons: One gun; 10,550kg (23,259 lb) of bombs

The F-22 Raptor is considered to be more cost effective than other stealth aircraft like the F-117 Nighthawk and the B-2 Spirit

JOINT STRIKE FIGHTER

The F-35 Joint Strike Fighter (JSF) is currently being developed jointly by the United States, Britain and many other partner countries. The Joint Strike Fighter will not only be used for tactical bombing but also for air-to-air combat. It is being designed on the same lines as the highly successful F-22 Raptor, only with better thrust vectoring capabilities.

Eurofighter Typhoon F2

Manufactured by: BAE Systems, U.K.
Crew: One or two
Maximum speed: 2,125 km/h (1,321 mph)
Weapons: One cannon; up to 6,500 kg (14,330 lb) of bombs and missiles

European effort

The most well known European combat aircraft projects are the Eurofighter and Rafale. Following the current trend of multi-role strike fighters, Britain, Germany, Italy and Spain jointly developed the Eurofighter Tyhoon. This fighter combines agility, stealth technology and performance, making it the best fighter aircraft; second only to the F-22 Raptor. The Rafale, belonging to the French Air Force and Navy, has also been developed as a multi-role fighter and has all the features of the Typhoon and F-22 Raptor.

The Eurofighter Typhoon is said to be as efficient and agile as the F-22 Raptor

The Joint Strike Fighter is expected to be more advanced than both the Eurofighter and the F-22 Raptor

F-35 Joint Strike Fighter

Manufactured by: Joint venture by Lockheed Martin Aeronautics and Northrop Grumman, U.S.A. and BAE Systems, U.K.
Crew: Single
Maximum speed: 2,250 km/h (1,398 mph)
Weapons: One cannon; bombs and missiles

GLOSSARY

Acceleration: The increase in the rate of speed of something

Aerial: Of or in the air

Aerodynamic: A shape that helps reduce the drag caused by air moving past it

Afterburners: An additional part in a jet aircraft that gives extra thrust during take-off or supersonic flight

Agile: Quick; lively; nimble

Air bag: A safety device fitted to cars that deploys a bag of air rapidly upon impact

Air superiority: The dominance of the air force of one country over the enemy during a war

Ammunition dumps: A military facility that stores weapons and explosives

Anti-lock Braking System: A system that transmits driver pressure on the brake pedal in a way that stops tyres from locking up

Asphalt: A brownish-black solid or semi-solid substance obtained usually as a by-product of petroleum. It is used as a waterproofing agent and to pave roads

Aviation: Of, or relating to aircraft

Axle: A central shaft between the wheels of a vehicle. It maintains the position of the wheels and also bears the weight of the vehicle and the extra load it carries

Backhoe: A deep, curved shovel-like tool attached to a long mechanical arm used for digging during construction works

Boom: The long mechanical arm of a construction vehicle that holds the main tool like a bucket in the case of a digger, or a hook in the case of a crane

Cc: Cubic centimetre: a metric unit of measurement used in relation to the size of a vehicle's engine

Ceramic brakes: High-performance disc brakes that can endure high temperatures and levels of wear

Chassis: The basic metallic framework of an automobile consisting of the engine, driveshaft, axles and suspension

Components: Parts

Coupe: A car with two doors and a fixed roof

Cruiser: Motorcycle meant for cruising purposes

Displacement: The quantity of fuel held by a fuel tank

Emissions: Gasses that are produced by the combustion engine and released through the exhaust

Ergonomic: Something that is designed for ease of use and comfort through its design

Exhaust: The parts of an engine that discharge waste gasses

Fixed wing aircraft: An aeroplane; any heavier-than-air craft that does not use its wings to generate power for flying

Fuselage: The main body of an aircraft that carries the crew and passengers or cargo

Gear box: An assembly of cogs that help transfer power from the engine to the wheels of a vehicle at a range of speeds

Grenade: A small bomb with a fuse that is usually thrown by hand or discharged from a rifle or a launcher

Guided missile: A missile that can seek out and follow its target

Horsepower (hp): A measurement of power

Impeller: A rotating device that forces a particular material in a

122

GLOSSARY

specific direction under pressure

Internal combustion engine: A heat engine in which the fuel burns in a closed space called the combustion chamber. The resulting high temperature and pressure cause the gases in the chamber to expand and in turn act on the pistons or rotors that move the vehicle

Landfill: A waste disposal site, where household rubbish and industrial waste is dumped into large pits and then covered with soil

Manoeuvre: To control direction or movement of something

Outrigger: A heavy projection that is actually an addition to the main structure of a vehicle meant to provide balance to the vehicle or to support another extension

Pneumatic tyres: Tyres that are filled with air. The air in such tyres act as shock absorber when the tyre goes over bumps on roads. These tyres are most commonly used in modern vehicles

Pontoon: A floating device that can be made from metal, concrete or rubber that is used to support aquatic vessels, bridges and certain land vehicles. Pontoons comprise watertight chambers filled with air

Propeller: A device consisting of blades attached to a shaft, the spinning of which propels a boat or an aircraft forward

Push-cat: A tracked dozer or any similar vehicle that pushes another vehicle like a scraper from behind in order to load the latter with hard material

Quarry: A type of mine from which rock or minerals can be extracted

Reconnaissance: Investigation survey

Retractable: Something that can be retracted or withdrawn; foldable

Simulation: A training programme or a real world event that is imitated by a computer programme

Snowplough: A device that helps to remove snow. A vehicle equipped with such a device is also called a snowplough

Sound barrier: The sudden increase in drag (air resistance) that an aircraft nearing supersonic speed experiences

Spoiler: A long and narrow plate on the upper surface of the rear part of the car giving downforce to the rear wheels at high speed

Squadron: An air-force unit made up of three or four flights consisting of 12-24 aircraft

Supercruise: Ability of certain aircraft to cruise at supersonic speeds without the help of afterburners

Surveillance: Observation Thrust vectoring – the ability of an aircraft to direct the thrust from its main engines either downwards or upwards

Suspension: The system of springs and shock absorbers by which a vehicle is cushioned from road conditions

Torque: The effect of force that causes an object to rotate in relation to the transfer of engine power to the wheels

Tourer: Motorcycle meant for touring purposes

Tracks: Road wheels surrounded by a chain made of alloy steel. Tracks are used instead of wheels in tanks and certain construction vehicles, as they distribute the weight of these vehicles over a larger area thereby preventing the vehicle from sinking into soft ground or snow

Unescorted: Unaccompanied

INDEX

acceleration 30, 45, 52, 58
aerodynamic 39, 43, 45
Active Camber Control System 23
aerodynamic 20, 26, 27
AH-64 Apache 117
Aichi D3A 101
all-wheel drive system 35
anti lock braking system 10
Avro Lancaster 98
AV-8B Harrier 113

B-1 Lancer 108
B-29 Superfortress Enola Gay 103
B-58 Hustler 108
Benz, Karl 7

carbon fibre 10, 18, 20, 22, 28
cc 39, 42, 43, 45, 49, 53, 55, 59, 61
ceramic brakes 35

CH-47 Chinook 116
CH-53E Super Stallion 116
CH-54 Skycrane 115
chassis 44, 45, 48, 57
cockpit 25, 29, 31, 34
components 38, 44, 59
console 53
cruiser 37, 51, 54, 55, 60, 63

Daimler, Gottlieb 61
deceleration 53
de Havilland DH-100 Vampire 104
displacement 46

electric car 11
Energy Storage System 11
embellish 45
emissions 49
English Electric Lightning 106
ergonomics 43, 46
Eurofighter Typhoon 121

exhaust 49, 62, 64

F-14 Tomcat 107
F-15A Eagle 112
F-22 Raptor 120
F-35 Joint Strike Fighter 121
F-100 Super Sabre 106
F-117 Nighthawk 110
Fisker, Henrik 30
Fokker, Anthony 96
Fokker D.VII 96
Fokker E-1 monoplane 96
fork 45, 55, 59, 63
fuel 37, 51, 53, 59

Garros, Roland 96
gasoline 7, 9, 19,
gearbox 24, 28, 35, 52, 53
Gumpert, Roland 28

handlebar 47, 55, 61
Hayabusa engine 20, 21
Heinkel **111** 98

INDEX

Hilderbrand and Wolfmuller 61
Hiroshima 103
HMS Hibernia 112
horsepower (hp) 45, 53, 55, 58

integrated 47, 59

Junkers Ju **87** 99

Kamikaze 101

lateral stability 23

manoeuvre 46, 47
Messerschmitt Me **262** 104, 105
Mi-24 118
Morane-Saulnier Type L 97

Nagasaki 103
navigation system 17
Nieuport **17** 97

P-36 Hawk 102

P-40 Warhawk 102
P-51 Mustang 102
P-80 Shooting Star 104
Pearl Harbour 100-101, 102
Pedersen, Mikkel Steen 20
Petlyakov **2** 99
pillion 47
powerplant 31, 35, 45, 52, 55, 57

Rafale 121

SA 341 Gazelle 119
Sea King 119
Sensotronic Brake Control System 24
SH-60 Sea Hawk 117
Sikorsky, Igor 114
Sikorsky XR-**4** 114
Sopwith 1 1/2 Strutter 97
spoiler 16, 26
stereo system 17
street-legal 65

Sukhoi Su-**27** 107
Sukhoi Su-30 MKI 110
Super Frelon 119
suspension 41, 43, 49, 55, 63

Terblanche, Pierre 42
testastretta 39, 41, 42, 43
torque 38, 50
tourer 60, 61
Tupolev Tu-22M 109
turbochargers 17

Vietnam War 106, 115

weight 38, 39, 62
Westland Lynx 118
windshield 55

xenon lamps 22

Yakovlev Yak-**15** 105
Yakovlev Yak-**38** 112